*"**Pearls of Wisdom** examines some of the most familiar and well-loved passages in the Bible. My friend, Mary Love Eyster, and her daughter, Weety Vickery, draw on years of teaching and life experience to share their wisdom. I would encourage you to use this study guide as a tool to teach teens how to apply these Scriptural principles to everyday life!"*

Josh D. McDowell
Author and Speaker

PEARLS OF WISDOM

IN HOME BIBLE STUDY FOR TEENS

MARY LOVE EYSTER, WEETY VICKERY

WESTBOW®
PRESS
A DIVISION OF THOMAS NELSON
& ZONDERVAN

Also by Mary Love Eyster and Weety Vickery
It Will Stand

Also by Mary Love Eyster
Love Notes
Life's Little Frustrations

Pearls of Wisdom: Student's Book

In Home Bible Study for Teens

MARY LOVE EYSTER, WEETY VICKERY

All Scriptures are taken from THE HOLY BIBLE, NEW INTERNATIONAL VERSION®, NIV® Copyright © 1973, 1978, 1984, 2011 by Biblica, Inc.® Used by permission. All rights reserved worldwide.

WestBow Press books may be ordered through booksellers or by contacting:

WestBow Press
A Division of Thomas Nelson & Zondervan
1663 Liberty Drive
Bloomington, IN 47403
www.westbowpress.com
1 (866) 928-1240

ISBN: 978-1-4908-4147-2 (sc)
ISBN: 978-1-4908-4146-5 (e)

Library of Congress Control Number: 2014911039

Printed in the United States of America.

WestBow Press rev. date: 06/25/2014

Table of Contents

PREFACE

Dear girls,

The aim of this book is to acquaint you in-depth with some of the most familiar and best loved passages in the Bible. We pray that you will be inspired to make wise choices by the book of Proverbs. As you study the Scriptures with your friends, we pray that this will create positive peer pressure during these crucial growing up years. The home setting gives an atmosphere of informality, which makes it easy for you to share with each other. Nothing seems to bring friends closer than studying God's word together. We pray that God's "pearls" become the most precious jewels in your life!

—Mary Love Eyster & Weety Vickery

INTRODUCTION TO PROVERBS

"The fear of the Lord is the beginning of wisdom." Proverbs 1:7

Certain clothes go in and out of style. It is said that if you keep out of date clothes long enough, they will eventually come back in style. Amazingly enough, even bell bottoms have recycled! Certain words are like fashion; their use comes in and out of style. We use them for a while and then they are dropped from our vocabularies. They are considered outdated or old fashioned. One of my grandfather's favorite words was "wholesome." I don't hear that word used much anymore. Another word I don't hear often is "wisdom." This is the key word in our study of Proverbs.

WIZBITS We have a collection of wise sayings in our society today, sayings that have been passed down orally from generation to generation. Some are based on Scripture; others have come from literature; some have come from observation. What *WIZBITS* can you recall? I'll get you started.

Two heads are better than _____.

Actions speak louder than _____.

All that glitters is not _____.

_____

_____

_____

Proverbs 1:1 ascribes its "wise words" to whom? _____

Most of the book of Proverbs is closely linked to Solomon. He was the son of King David and Bathsheba. He inherited the kingdom when his father David died.

Read I Kings 3:5-13. This passage of Scripture gives us important insight into Solomon's wisdom. God appeared to Solomon in a dream.   God instructed Solomon to ask for whatever he wanted, and it would be granted.

What would you ask for?

What did Solomon request?

Just how much wisdom did God grant Solomon? I Kings 4:29, I Kings 4:32

The book of Proverbs encourages EVERYONE to get wisdom.   Gaining wisdom should be a top priority for us--just as it was for Solomon.

Proverbs 2:2

Proverbs 3:21

Proverbs 13:12

Wisdom was the number one priority for Solomon, and he tells everyone in Proverbs just how important wisdom is in life.

Proverbs 16:16

Proverbs 3:13-15

Apparently, Solomon believed obtaining wisdom is of more importance than obtaining _____.

Charles Swindoll said, "Foolish indeed is the person who considers himself safe and sound because he has money….Money, in the final analysis, brings no lasting satisfaction, certainly not in the area of things that really matter. There are many things that no amount of money can buy. Think of it this way:

Money can buy medicine, but not health.

Money can buy a house, but not a home.

Money can buy companionship, but not friends.

Money can buy food, but not an appetite.

Money can buy a bed, but not sleep.

Money can buy the good life, but not eternal life.

It is God alone who is able to supply us with all things to enjoy."

We are truly wealthy when we learn that the greatest gifts ever obtained are the ones that only God can give. What "treasures" might you gain in an obedient life to him?

LESSON 2

THE BENEFITS OF WISDOM

"He who cherishes understanding prospers." Proverbs 19:8

In our last lesson, we learned that we are to incline our ears to wisdom, preserve sound judgment, and apply our hearts to instruction. We learned that it is better to have wisdom than wealth. Like Solomon, obtaining wisdom should be at the top of our list of desires.

In this lesson, we will look at the benefits of having Godly wisdom and the consequences of relying on human wisdom alone.

What benefits of having wisdom do the following verses convey to us?

Proverbs 3:16-18

Proverbs 2:11-12

Proverbs 3:12

Proverbs 3:7b-8

Proverbs 19:8b

Proverbs 24:5

Proverbs 24:14

Proverbs 3:5-6

Solomon not only commented on the benefits of Godly wisdom, but he also discussed the consequences of folly and warned us over and over about the results of relying on human wisdom alone. What are some of those results found in the following verses?

Proverbs 24:19-20

KEY TO SUCCESS

Each of you has already experienced or will encounter hardships and unfamiliar terrain in your life. The key to your success is learning to walk by faith and not by sight.

Proverbs 5:22-23

Many people flirt with temptation, believing they can rescue themselves at any time, but they wind up being caught in evil and suffering the consequences of their folly. Can you think of any examples?

There once was an eagle perched on a block of ice above Niagara Falls. The swift current was rapidly carrying the ice and its passenger close to the edge. Other birds warned the eagle of the danger ahead, but he replied, "I have great, powerful wings, and I can fly off my perch any time I please." When the edge of the falls was only a few feet away, the eagle spread his wings to mount up, only to discover that his claws had become frozen to the block of ice.

Where can I get this kind of great wisdom?

Proverbs 1:7

Proverbs 2:6

James 1:5

Psalm 111:10

If we are going to walk by God's wisdom, we must have a **_teachable spirit_**. What do you think this means?

Proverbs 9:7-9

Proverbs 12:1

Proverbs 12:15

There seems to be more advice out there than there are those who are seeking it! Have you seen restaurants or businesses that solicit your opinion with survey cards or even post 1-800 numbers for feedback? What eagerness they are showing to improve their products and serve the public better. What eagerness to listen, to learn, and to grow! Then I ask myself, do I have that kind of attitude toward God and others? Am I eager to provide better service to people in Christ's name, to have my weaknesses and faults pointed out so that I might grow? Am I ready to take criticism, suggestions, and advice? A teachable spirit and an eagerness to learn are marks of true wisdom. The next time that we feel so quick to defend ourselves when criticized, regardless of who is giving the advice, stop and pray, "Lord, are you giving me a bit of gentle advice that I need to hear?"

ROOM FOR IMPROVEMENT IS THE

LARGEST ROOM IN THE WORLD

You can have Godly wisdom if you choose to have an intimate relationship with his Son. Knowing him in a personal way is our direct path to the wisdom of God. We can choose to seek God's wisdom or we can rely on our own human ability-it's our choice. However, we will reap the consequences of our decision.

LESSON 3

PROVERBS—FAMILY LIFE

Family life is the topic of our lesson today. Solomon gave us some of his great wisdom for dealing with family situations. He specifically talked about husband-wife and parent-child relationships, but many of his principles can be applied to all kinds of family relationships.

Solomon emphasized faithfulness and purity in marriage for the men, warning several times not to become involved with adulteresses. His warning to be faithful to one's spouse in marriage could be written to women also, because faithfulness is basic in a successful and happy marriage.

Proverbs 27:8

Proverbs 6:27-29

Proverbs 5:15-18

Why is marriage hard, and why do you feel so many marriages today do not last?

My grandmother had a great statement, "I work on my marriage every day." Men and women change through the years. It takes effort to keep a marriage fresh! I have found that keeping a close walk with God helps more than anything else.

Psalm 127:1a

Proverbs 14:1

Proverbs 24:3-4 paints a beautiful picture of a harmonious marriage and family, "By wisdom a house is built, and through understanding it is established; through knowledge its rooms are filled with rare and beautiful treasures."

There are no treasures on earth more beautiful to me

than the members of my family.

Solomon had instructions for children also. Read the following verses and record their advice.

Proverbs 4:1

Proverbs 1:8-9

Proverbs 3:1-2

At every age we can remember and profit from the things our parents have taught us.

Proverbs 19:27

If children are to heed the instruction of parents, it goes without saying that parents must give their children wise instruction to remember.   Other family members such as grandparents and aunts and uncles can contribute important instruction and impart wisdom as well. Would you like to tell of someone in your life who has shared his or her wisdom with you?

Satan would love nothing more than to destroy homes. He would delight in having everyone looking out for his or her interests only. He would love our mindset to be, "What would I like most?" "What can others do for me?" "I will see what kind of pleasure I can obtain from others." In other words, he wants you to be a "taker" instead of a "giver."

"Only be careful, and watch yourselves closely so that you do not forget the things your eyes have seen or let them slip from your heart as long as you shall live." Deuteronomy 4:9

As a young woman, you need to consider your future and the home you will have one day. Have you been taught things that you will want to pass on to your children? Did the values that your parents instilled in you come from their parents, your grandparents? Will you be passing them along to your children's children one day? Have you stopped to think that what you teach your children could affect many generations of people?   This is your legacy!

How can you raise children who will bring you pleasure?

Proverbs 29:3

Proverbs 22:6

Proverbs 23:13-14

Proverbs 13:24

Parents shouldn't make excuses for their children's bad behavior.

Proverbs 20:11

Even very young children know if what they are doing is right or wrong!

> *Abraham Lincoln once said,*
>
> *"No one is poor who had a godly mother."*

A functional family of peaceful relationships is of greatest importance, not only to us as individuals but to future generations.   Our family role may be our most rewarding role in life.

FRIENDSHIPS AND RELATIONSHIPS

Relationships with other people can be the source of our greatest joy on earth, our deepest sorrow, or our greatest irritation. But our relationships with other people are of utmost importance in our lives. It's a wonderful thing to share the most intimate parts of our life with a trustworthy friend who has our best interests at heart.

Proverbs cautions us to choose the right kinds of friends, to select our friends and companions with great care.

Proverbs 12:26

Proverbs 13:20

Proverbs 14:7

Proverbs 24:1-2

We need to choose friends who are good for us, who help us to be better people.

When I was a teenager, my mother used to pray, not only for me but also for my friends, because she knew how much influence they had on my life.

Proverbs 27:17

That is the kind of friendship we should cultivate!

Proverbs warns us not to stir up dissention or quarrel with each other. The following Scriptures have some interesting word pictures.

Proverbs 30:33

Proverbs 17:14

Proverbs 12:16

Proverbs 19:11

Proverbs 17:9

True friends are loyal friends. They have integrity. They can be trusted. They are dependable. They are truthful.

Proverbs 27:10

Proverbs 25:19

Proverbs 12:22

Proverbs 24:28

If a person tells you somebody else's business, that person will tell your business to somebody else.

Proverbs 11:9a

Proverbs 11:12-13

Proverbs 25:9

In only 20 years, the spread of HIV/AIDS has grown from 8 million cases to 34 million cases worldwide. The spread of "spiritual sickness", through gossip, can travel just as fast. It can be quite damaging to individuals, friends, families and churches. Each of us should be careful not to spread the sickness of gossip.

To silence gossip, refuse to repeat it. Is this a "natural" tendency?

Proverbs 26:20 "Without wood a fire goes out; without gossip a quarrel dies down."
>   Wisdom is knowing when to speak your mind and when to mind your speech.
>   It takes a wise person to know what not to say—and then not to say it!
>   If you hold your tongue at the right time, you won't have to eat your words later.

From **The Daily Bread**, "An elderly gentleman tells this story: 'One day when I was about 8 years of age, I was playing beside an open window while our neighbor confided to my mother a serious problem concerning another person. When our visitor was gone, my mother realized I had heard everything said. 'If Mrs. Brown had left her purse here just now, would you give it to someone else?' 'Why of course not,' I replied. 'Well, she left something more precious than that. The story she told could hurt many people and cause much unhappiness. It still belongs to her, and we shall not pass it on to anyone. Do you understand?' I did, and I have remembered ever since that a confidence or a bit of careless gossip is not mine to distribute to others."

George Washington Carver once said, "How far you go in life depends on your being tender with the young, compassionate with the aged, sympathetic with the striving, and tolerant of the weak and the strong. Because someday in life you will have been all of these."

Proverbs 16:24

Proverbs 25:11

Proverbs 15:23

Proverbs 12:25

What a joy it is to see the face of a friend brighten from timely words or advice!

Some people have a special gift of encouragement. Do you know someone in your group who has this trait?

A good memory verse:

Proverbs 17:17 "A friend loves at all times,

and a brother is born for adversity."

Proverbs 18:24

Jesus is the best friend we will ever have. Other friends may disappoint us, let us down, fail to care about us, turn their backs on us, or walk off and leave us, but Jesus will always care, always understand, and always be there for us. He is the ultimate model of what a friend should be like, and of what we should be like as friends. He is the *ultimate* friend for each of us!

POWER, PROVIDENCE, PRINCIPLES

Have you ever shown interest in an activity that you didn't really care about just to connect and spend time with a person who enjoyed that activity?   In some cases, we step out of our comfort zone to win the approval of others.

We have a heavenly Father who loves us, and, hopefully, we love him so much that we want his approval and want to do things that bring pleasure to him. Surely, we will likewise want to avoid doing those things that would displease God, things that would make him sad or disappointed in us.   This lesson talks about living wisely in the fear of the Lord.   When we speak about fearing the Lord, we simply mean reverencing him, living to please him, avoiding what displeases him, putting him first, and coming into alignment with his will.

Three ways we can do that:
1. We accept his **power**, his sovereignty, and his plan for our lives.
2. We acknowledge his **providence** and are grateful for his daily protection and provision.
3. We act on his **precepts and principles**, applying the things we learn in his word.

His Power

It pleases God when we accept his plan and his sovereignty, his power and his control. God is our creator. He has a plan for all of his creation, including you and me, and he has the power to fulfill his plans. He has given us a free will with which we can make many decisions in our lives, but our free will operates under the umbrella of God's sovereignty.

When I took a recent cruise, I was able to move around the ship and choose activities of my liking.   All the while I was going about my sunning, games, eating, etc., the ship was on its predetermined course to the next port. So it is with God's sovereignty and man's freedom. They exist together.

God's sovereignty can overrule the freedom of man at any time!

Proverbs 19:21

Proverbs 21:30

Proverbs 27:1

Acknowledging the sovereignty of God includes acknowledging the frailty of man. If we are honest in our comparison of man with God, we will have a spirit of great humility because we are totally dependent upon our creator. Some people may look big and important compared to some other people, but how small we must look when compared to an eternal, all powerful, all wise God, creator of this vast universe and everything in it! **How awesome God is!!!**

PSALM 104 (selected readings)

"O Lord my God, how great you are! You are robed with honor and with majesty and light! You stretched out the starry curtain of the heavens and hollowed out the surface of the earth to form the seas. The clouds are your chariots. You ride upon the wings of the wind. The angels are your messengers...You bound the world together so that it would never fall apart....You spoke, and at the sound of your shout the water collected into vast ocean beds, and mountains rose and valleys sank to the levels you decreed. And then you set a boundary for the seas, so that they would never again cover the earth. You placed springs in the valleys, and streams that gush from the mountains. They give water for all the animals to drink....You send rain upon the mountains and fill the earth with fruit. The tender grass grows up at your command to feed the cattle, and there are fruit trees, vegetables, and grain for man to cultivate.... You assigned the moon to mark the months, and the sun to mark the days....In your wisdom you have made them all! The earth is full of your riches."

Prideful people can disbelieve or resent the thought of God's control, but the adventure of the Christian life is in knowing that God desires to involve us, to allow us to partner with him and to be a part of his plan. Some people will only accept the reality that God is in control when it becomes abundantly clear that we are not, when some disaster occurs in our lives.

Proverbs 3:7

Proverbs 8:13b

Pride is the only disease known to man that makes everyone sick except the person who has it!

When I acknowledge God's place as first in my life, he directs the course of my life to align with his purposes.

Romans 8:28

Christian author, James Dobson, wrote: "Whenever I am tempted to become self-important and authoritative, I'm reminded of what the mother whale said to her baby: when you get to the top and start to blow, that's when you get harpooned!"

His Providence

It also pleases God when we acknowledge his providence. This is when his loving hand breaks through time and circumstances to give help or direction to his children. He doesn't just sit up in heaven and watch us struggle.

God knew he planned to flood the earth, so he told Noah to build the ark before it started raining. He parted the sea for Moses and the Israelites when they arrived on the shore with the Egyptian army behind them. He put Joseph in an influential position in anticipation of the famine. He closed the lions' mouths for Daniel. These saints trusted that God was working out his plan and providing for them even if their circumstances appeared for awhile to suggest otherwise. Have any of you come through a hard situation and later looked back and realized that God had been with you?

1 Thessalonians 5:18

When the direction of our lives is interrupted, even if it seems unexpected or catastrophic, it may simply be a course adjustment from our heavenly Father, pointing us back toward his plan. We can rest assured that he is still directing our course. In his providence, he will provide whatever we need to go through any situation. He will always be there for us. He will never forsake us.

Soon after the death of my father, my mother was diagnosed with cancer. I sat with her through several of her "all day" chemotherapy treatments. Sometimes I saw things only with "earthly eyes". I had much anxiety and fear of losing my other parent. My mother's attitude would always bring me back. She

J.I. Packer from Knowing God, "What matters supremely is not, in the last analysis, the fact that I know God, but the larger fact which underlies it—that He knows me. I am graven on the palms of His hands. All my knowledge of Him depends on His sustained initiative in knowing me. I know Him because He first knew me, and continues to know me. He knows me as a friend, one who loves me; and there is no moment when His eye is off me, or His attention distracted from me, and no moment, therefore, when His care falters. There is unspeakable comfort in knowing that God is constantly taking knowledge of me in love and watching over me for my good."

was kind to all who treated her. She never "fretted" or even cried about her situation. She has been a Christian many years and has a close relationship with God. When I asked her how she could be so calm and accepting she said, "I have walked with the Lord a long time and I am not going to quit now; I want to do this well."

His Precepts and Principles

It pleases God when we act on his precepts and principles. Wisdom is knowing which path to take. Integrity is taking it.

Proverbs 15:9

Proverbs 4:11

Proverbs 21:21

Precepts are black and white, do or don't, statements or commands. Principles involve judgment calls. An example of a precept is a sign that says "Speed Limit 35 MPH." But "Drive Carefully" is a principle, since it can vary with road or traffic conditions. The more we know about God's word, the better judgment calls or decisions we can make.

What principles and precepts have we learned so far in Proverbs? What applications do we need to make in our lives? Here is a summary of the main points.

Get _____.

Trust and _____ God.

Work _____. Be diligent.

Prepare for the _____.

Be honest. Tell the _____. Be a person of integrity.

Be humble and teachable. Profit from _____.

Listen to the instruction of your _____.

Be faithful to your _____. Don't gossip.

Don't quarrel. Overlook and _____offenses.

Be _____ to other people.

When we acknowledge God and try to please him, he will give us direction and his wisdom. James 3:17 tells us what our lives will be like. "But the wisdom that comes from heaven is first of all pure; then peace-loving, considerate, submissive, full of mercy and good fruit, impartial and sincere."

WORK, MONEY AND HONESTY

Do you think God is interested in your "day to day" life? Does he really care if you do well in school and keep your room neat? Is he interested in the way you handle your allowance/money? Is he interested in how you interact with people you see on a daily basis; your teachers, friends and family members?

To say "no" to these questions is to relegate God to a place of little or no importance.   To say "yes" to these questions transforms whatever you do into a thing of dignity, high purpose, satisfaction, and excitement.

Ted Engstrom, from The Making of A Christian Leader, "The world needs men who cannot be bought; whose word is their bond; who put character above wealth; who possess opinions and a will; who are larger than their vocations; who do not hesitate to take chances; who will not lose their individuality in a crowd; who will be as honest in small things as in great things; who will make no compromise with wrong; whose ambitions are not confined to their own selfish desires; who will not say they do it 'because everybody else does it'; who are true to their friends through good report and evil report, in adversity as well as in prosperity; who do not believe that shrewdness, cunning and hardheadedness are the best qualities for winning success; who are not ashamed or afraid to stand for the truth when it is unpopular; who say 'no' with emphasis, although the rest of the world says 'yes.'"

There are three characteristics that are greatly desired in work situations according to Proverbs: honesty, hard work, and kindness to others. There are a number of verses that challenge us to be honest in our work relationships.

Proverbs 20:10

Proverbs 20:23

Proverbs 11:1

Proverbs 16:8

If your desire is to be a "fruit bearer", you must be honest! God knows when you have maneuvered, schemed and lied to get to the top.

The father says: "I want an explanation and I want the truth." The daughter replies: "Make up your mind, Dad; you can't have both!"

Proverbs 22:1

There are also many verses in Proverbs that emphasize the value of hard work and warn against laziness. (Proverbs refers to the lazy person as a "sluggard." This is a person who refuses to work!)

David Jeremiah wrote, "Billy Graham tells this of his upbringing: 'I was taught that laziness was one of the worst evils, and there was dignity and honor in labor. I could abandon myself enthusiastically to milking the cows, cleaning out the latrines, and shoveling manure, not because they were pleasant jobs, but because sweaty labor held its own satisfaction.' Through godly rearing, Billy Graham developed the valuable character quality of diligence. A diligent man is one who works hard at every task, no matter how important or how menial. He uses his time efficiently and always puts forth his best work…..Against the backdrop of people who avoid work, cut corners, and do half-hearted jobs, a diligent man stands out. Practicing diligence is an excellent way to stand out for Christ at home, in the workplace, and even at church. Today, complete each one of your tasks, however big or small, with diligence."

Proverbs 26:14-15

Proverbs 13:4

Proverbs 21:25-26

Proverbs 6:6-11

Proverbs 20:13

Proverbs 19:15

The best way to hear money jingle in your pocket is to shake a leg!
Proverbs 10:4-5

Proverbs 20:4

The sluggard will not even care for what he has and will make excuses!
Proverbs 12:27

Proverbs 19:24

Proverbs 22:13

The diligent man is rewarded with the fruit of his labors!
Proverbs 27:18a

Proverbs 18:20

Proverbs 21:5

Sometimes if we faithfully fulfill small tasks that God gives us, he will later promote us to larger ones. David cared for his flock of sheep as a boy and later rose to be King of Israel. Joshua was Moses' helper and later led the Israelites into the Promised Land. Abraham was obedient to God early on, and later God made him the father of his great nation.

Proverbs 14:23

"The world is full of willing people: some willing to work and the rest willing to let them."

Proverbs 28:19

Proverbs 24:27

Not only should we be diligent to take care of ourselves and our families but, if we are good workers, we should have enough to share with those less fortunate, and God expects us to be generous with others. Certainly he has been much more than generous with us. He has given us so many good gifts and lavished his love and grace on us!

Proverbs 11:16

Proverbs 14:31

Proverbs 28:27

Remember, if you commit your work to the Lord you will succeed.

Proverbs 13:7

Thomas Edison

"I never did anything worth doing by accident, nor did any of my inventions come by accident; they came by work." He also said, "Opportunity is missed by most people because it is dressed in overalls and looks like work."

LESSON 7

INTRODUCTION TO ECCLESIASTES

God included a vast array of people and situations in the Bible. Isn't that encouraging to us as we compare our lives to theirs? We can relate when we see them "rejoicing in the Lord" and we can also relate when we see them struggle. In the book of Ecclesiastes, we see Solomon at his lowest point. This is in contrast to Proverbs where he shared his incredible wisdom.

How many of you have experienced "down times" in your life?

Solomon's purpose in Ecclesiastes was to unlock the mysteries of life. One thousand years before Christ, he was searching for the answers to the big questions people have asked throughout history and are still asking today:
1. Who am I?
2. Where did I come from?
3. Why am I here?
4. Where am I going?
5. Is there meaning to life?
6. Is there a God?
7. Is there life after death?
8. Is life worth living? There are many people who don't think so and who attempt suicide every year. About 10% of those who try actually succeed.

The Declaration of Independence says a person should have the right to "life, liberty, and the pursuit of happiness." Most people pursue happiness in this life. Most want the richest and most fulfilling life they can possibly have. I do. Don't you?

The world offers us much pleasure and temporary satisfaction, but all roads, except

> Christian author Max Lucado writes, "Mine deep enough in every heart and you'll find it; a longing for meaning, a quest for purpose. As surely as a child breathes, he will someday wonder, 'What is the purpose of my life?'"

one, are dead end streets as far as answering the ultimate questions in life and giving us eternal joy and purpose. Many people are frustrated and are fighting a losing battle because they are trying to find happiness in places where it cannot be found. There is only one right road that leads to lasting joy.

Blaise Pascal, mathematician, physicist, and philosopher said, "There is a God shaped vacuum in the heart of every person that cannot be filled by any created thing but only by the creator himself." Nothing else in our life will satisfy like God.

With what things do we try to satisfy ourselves? How long does the satisfaction last? King Solomon tried most of the roads that people travel to try to find happiness, meaning and purpose. He came to the conclusion that these things could only be found in a relationship with God. Let's take a look at some of the roads he traveled.

Look at Ecclesiastes chapter one. In verse two, the author said that everything is *meaningless*. Solomon described the futility of life. The phrase "meaningless" expresses the sad belief that life is worthless. He gave us four reasons to support that conclusion.

MEANINGLESS

HAVING NO MEANING;
LACKING ANY SIGNIFICANCE

(These are found in Chapters 1 &2)

Life is boring.

Death is certain.

Wisdom is hopeless.

Wealth is futile.

In Chapter 1:3-10 Solomon talked about the monotony of life. What does this mean to you?

_____

_____

_____

_____

Everything has been tried. We bore easily. This is one reason I enjoy my grand-children so much. It is so much fun to see them experience things for the first time, things that no longer hold the same level of excitement for me.

What phrase does Solomon repeat often? _____. This phrase expresses the effort to find everything man needs in **this world**, the human point of view. Things look very different when you see them from God's point of view.

In verse 11 Solomon stated a theme that is echoed throughout this book; death is certain. We are born. We live. We die. Time will roll on, and we will be forgotten. That is life under the sun. **Without God,** this is the sum total of man's hope and future. But **with God**, what wonderful possibilities open up and give us hope for an incredible future with him.

> I said to myself, "Let's go for it—experiment with pleasure, have a good time!" But there was nothing to it, nothing but smoke.
>
> What do I think of the fun-filled life? Insane! Insane!
> My verdict on the pursuit of happiness? Who needs it?
>
> *Ecclesiastes 2:1-2 (The Message)*

Next Solomon explored the road of wisdom. Remember that God had given him a gigantic portion of wisdom, so if anyone could solve the mysteries of life by human wisdom, it should have been Solomon. But he showed that man's wisdom is limited!

Read Ecclesiastes 1:12-18.

Contrary to human thinking, education will not give man the answers he is seeking to the ultimate questions of life. No amount of human striving can explain life's meaning and purpose.

The next road Solomon went down was pleasure.

Read Ecclesiastes 2:1-2

Read Ecclesiastes 2:10

But that also proved to be meaningless. As a teen you might be thinking, "If I just had the right boyfriend, everything would be great." Many times the new wears off. He might make you mad or no longer be as exciting, and you may even break up. People are not perfect; only God is. We should look to God to fill us with peace, joy and satisfaction. God uses people and things to bring us a certain level of happiness, but contentment and abiding joy come from our relationship with God.

Many people go down the road of partying and entertainment. Solomon tried that too. Read Ecclesiastes 2:3

Solomon also tried the road of building projects, of hard work. Read Ecclesiastes 2:4-6

Solomon tried the road to wealth. Read Ecclesiastes 2:7-8a

It is good to have the things that money can buy, but don't lose the things that money can't buy!

Solomon had extreme wealth, beyond anything we could ever imagine. And yet even all that prosperity failed to satisfy him. It has been well said that despair rises out of circumstances of plenty rather than poverty. It is interesting that people who have less of the luxuries and pleasures of life still have the hope that if they had more life would be great.   And those who have an abundance of everything the world has to offer realize that it cannot give man inner peace and contentment. Another way to say it might be: the more we have, the more we want, and the more discontented we can become!

Tommy Nelson, in his commentary A Life Well Lived Study Guide: An In-depth Study of Ecclesiastes, said, "If ever there was a man who could find meaning outside of God, it was Solomon. In terms of intelligence, industry, and accomplishments, he had it all. Solomon used these gifts to accumulate wealth, discover knowledge, and experience pleasure. And he didn't do it in moderation but excess. If Solomon couldn't discover the secret to life, it can't be done. "

After Solomon had tried all these things, what was his conclusion about their value?

Read Ecclesiastes 2:10b-11

Read Ecclesiastes 2:17

Read Ecclesiastes 2:24-25

This lament of Solomon's goes on through chapter 7; then, a turning point occurs in Ecclesiastes 8:12 which says, "Yet surely I know that it shall be well with them that fear God." This is followed up in Ecclesiastes 12:13 which reads, "Fear God, and keep his commandments: for this is the whole duty of man."

When you are feeling down or defeated with your life, open your Bible to Ecclesiastes. There are 12 chapters of pure struggle, written for you, from the wisest man who ever lived. Perhaps you can find parallels in your own hard times and realize that you ARE NOT ALONE. Everyone goes through dark hours, but REJOICE because God is with you! It is in knowing God through Jesus Christ that we find true meaning, purpose and contentment in life and have the hope of an eternal future in heaven.

If you look to people and
things to satisfy you –
you end up distressed,

If you look to circumstances
for contentment -
you end up depressed,

But when you look to God to
fill you – you will be blessed!

GOD'S TIME
Ecclesiastes 3:1-14

In the book of Ecclesiastes, Solomon described the emptiness of life apart from God. No matter how random things may seem, in good times or bad, when you can't figure it out, you can take comfort in the truth. God has **a plan for your life**!

GOD IS AT WORK ALL THE TIME

In Ecclesiastes Chapter 3, Solomon clearly stated that God has a plan and does not waver from it. He is the one who has made the appointed time for everything. Solomon began with the familiar verses about the major events and seasons of life by declaring that all human experiences have a place in God's plan – birth, death, laughter, tears, war and peace.

Read Ecclesiastes 3:1-8

Ecclesiastes 3:1 "There is a time for everything, and everything of earth has its

_____."

Times and seasons are a regular part of life. From before our birth to the moment of our death, God is accomplishing his divine purpose. Ecclesiastes 8:6a "For there is a proper time and procedure for every matter."

Ecclesiastes 3:2a "There is a time to be _____ and a time to _____.

Have you ever thought it might be fun to live in another time period? Our birth and death are not happenstance. They are divine appointments. We live in this generation by his perfect timing. We were born into our specific family by God's plan.

> *Evangelist Billy Graham said, "Life is brief, and it can end in an instant. That's why we must never take life for granted but see every minute as a gift from God to be used for His glory."*

Read Psalm 139:16

Ecclesiastes 3:2b   "There is a time to

_____ and a time to _____."

Planting and harvesting make an interesting parallel to birth and death. A successful farmer must do both according to the seasons. He knows nature works for him only if he works with nature. Who can give an example of a gardening "rule of thumb?"

The secret to a successful life is to learn God's principles and cooperate with them.

Ecclesiastes 3:3 "There is a time to _____

and a time to _____."

Life seems to take place somewhere between a battlefield and a first aid station! When do you think it is an appropriate time to kill?

Ecclesiastes 3:4 "There is a time to _____ and a time to _____. There is a

time to be _____ and a time to _____."

These emotions should always be used at the appropriate time. They are used to show others your reaction to a situation. How much fun is it to share a laugh with friends when they are happy?   How consoling is it to have a friend share your sadness or your tears?

Read Proverbs 10:11

Read Proverbs 15:4

Read Proverbs 26:20

Ecclesiastes 3:5a "There is a time to _____ stones and a time to

_____ them."   A farmer will need to dispose of small stones when cultivating his field.   He might gather the larger ones and keep them to build fences or buildings.   This example of "sorting" can be used in many areas of life. Can you think of an example?

Ecclesiastes 3:5b "There is a time to hug and a time not to hug."

Ecclesiastes 3:6a "There is a time to _____ and a time to _____." Some translations say "to give up as lost."

Why would you decide this?

Ecclesiastes 3:6b "There is a time to _____ and a time to _____." Have you ever seen the show "Hoarders?"   We need to be wise in finding the right time to get rid of things.

Ecclesiastes 3:7a "There is a time to _____ and a time to _____." The Jews tore their clothing in times of grief. Joel 2:13 "Rend your heart and not your garments and turn unto the Lord."   God expects us to have sorrow during bereavement but not like unbelievers, who have no hope.   There also comes a time to "get over it" and sew it up!

Ecclesiastes 3:7b "There is a time to _____ and a time to _____." If God has told you to be silent you need to heed his advice. There are also times you need to speak up!

Ecclesiastes 3:8 "There is a time to _____ and a time to _____." There are some times that even Christians are to hate. Psalm 97:10 "Let those who love the Lord hate evil."   Read Proverbs 6:16-19. Find seven things that God hates. (Hatred should be aimed at the sin, not the sinner.)

1.

2.

3.

4.

5.

6.

7.

"There is a time for _____ and a time for _____."   When would a time for war be appropriate?

Read Ecclesiastes 3:9-14

What did Solomon share in these verses that he concluded about life?

We see the ugly cocoon – God sees the beautiful butterfly. We see today – he's working on forever. He makes everything beautiful in its time – your loss, your heartaches, your trials, your battles, your illnesses, and your failures.

Write Romans 8:28

How can hard times or sad times work for our good?

We should not portray the Christian life as "smooth sailing" all the time. The Bible tells us that our lives will be seasons of ups and downs.

God is wise! Even bad things can be used to help us become the Christians he created us to be!

LESSON 9

THE BEATITUDES
Matthew 5:1-12

All people pursue happiness. Some look to the entertainment industry--movies, theater, television and sports. Others may search for happiness in food and drink. Some spend money, and some travel to acquire happiness. Still others look to their boyfriends or partners for their joy. That kind of happiness brings temporary satisfaction. Jesus pointed to a source of lasting happiness. In the Sermon on the Mount, he listed some spiritual qualities that characterize the truly happy person. Believers find these qualities in a life of submission, trust, obedience, and faithfulness to God. Happiness depends on what we **are**, not on what we have or what we do or where we go!

Jesus told us the inward qualities that should be found in the life of a Christian in his much loved sermon. The word "beatitude" means "blessing" and comes from the Latin word for blessed. Blessed means "how happy," "how fortunate," and "to be congratulated." The beatitudes are the attitudes that ought to be in our lives if we are true Christians.

be·at·i·tude

noun \bē-ˈa-tə-ˌtüd, -ˌtyüd\

Etymology: derived from Latin *beatus* "happy, blessed"

Definition: 1: a state of utmost bliss

2: any of the declarations made in the Sermon on the Mount (Matthew 5:3-11) beginning "Blessed are"

Do you think there are people today who "pretend" to be holy? People whose walk doesn't match their talk?

Who were the Pharisees?

The Pharisees emphasized outward behavior, but Jesus emphasized the inner attitudes and motives of the heart. The Pharisees and teachers of the law kept the **letter of the law**, but Jesus showed by his life and his teachings that keeping the **spirit of the law** is much more important.

Read Matthew 5:1-3

The "poor in spirit" are those who are humble, who realize how weak and sinful they are. They know that they are spiritually bankrupt apart from Christ and realize how spiritually wealthy they are with him. Their attitude is just the opposite of the proud, self-sufficient, self-righteous attitude of the Scribes and Pharisees. As a reward, the poor in spirit receive the kingdom of heaven. Because they recognize and acknowledge their need for God's power and sovereignty in their lives, they receive it. God accepts and directs people who express their need of him and commit their lives to him.

SELF EXAMINE—Is this an area in your life that could use some work? Do you humbly and submissively come to God for help or do you try to make it under your own power?

_____

_____

_____

Read Matthew 5:4

The mourning in this verse is a sincere sorrow for sin, the kind of sorrow that leads to repentance. God forgives and comforts us when we approach him in true repentance. Peter mourned with a true godly sorrow and was forgiven. Judas had only a worldly kind of sorrow, regret without repentance, and took his own life.

SELF EXAMINE—When you ask God for forgiveness, are you just trying to "get out of trouble" or make yourself "feel better" or are you deeply disturbed that you have disconnected your fellowship with God by sinning?

_____

_____

_____

Read Matthew 5:5

Meekness is not weakness. The word translated "meek" was used by the Greeks to describe a horse that had been broken. It refers to power under control. Meekness means not asserting our own rights but living for the glory of God. It is the opposite of self will.

SELF EXAMINE—Think of a time that you gave up your own right (or desire) to live for the glory of God. Share if you like.

_____

_____

_____

Read Matthew 5:6

A true Christian has an appetite for spiritual things. There's no reason to let our hunger for spiritual nourishment go unsatisfied! Christ, the Bread of Life, satisfies our spiritual hunger when we come to him and feast on his word!

SELF EXAMINE—Do you have a deep longing to spend time with God through regular prayer and Bible reading? (Don't forget you are involved in this study!)

_____

_____

_____

Read Matthew 5:7

This is the law of the harvest--we reap what we sow. God has been faithful to show us mercy in saving us when we were sinners. He expects us to pass the mercy of forgiveness along to others.

SELF EXAMINE—Is there someone you need to forgive? Remember what you ask in the Lord's Prayer: forgive me my trespasses as I forgive those that trespass against me!

_____

_____

_____

Read Matthew 5:8

The person who is pure in heart has a single heart. His heart is not divided between God and the world.   His heart has unmixed motives and focuses on devotion to God.   The person who is focused on God above all else will be able to see his heavenly Father in a unique way.

SELF EXAMINE—If you were to honestly examine your devotion to God, what percentage of your heart would you say he possesses?

_____

_____

_____

Read Matthew 5:9

Peace makers are not simply peace lovers. They are involved in resolving conflicts. They are part of the solution, not the problem. Sometimes this takes risk, and, as a peacemaker, you might be injured in the crossfire. Peacemakers take the risk and stay with the job because they want to serve and honor God.

Read Matthew 5:10-12

How do you react to opposition in your Christian life? You can become a martyr and feel sorry for yourself. You can become angry and fight back. You can react in fear and back away from any public stand for Christ. But true righteousness stands firm in the face of opposition and discovers that God's powerful presence strengthens and sustains us if we exhibit the courage to speak up on his behalf.

SELF EXAMINE—Am I able to stand boldly for Christ during opposition to him? Do I have the scriptural knowledge needed to make an adequate response/ defense?

_____

_____

_____

The Holy Spirit enables us to experience the true righteousness expressed in the Beatitudes in our daily lives. This does not mean that we live sinless, perfect lives. What it does mean is that, if we yield ourselves completely to him, Christ will live his life through us by the power of his Spirit. The only way we can experience this true righteousness is through the power of Jesus Christ. The Beatitudes give us a clear picture of what a true disciple of Christ should be like.

JESUS TAUGHT US TO PRAY
Matthew 6

In the last chapter, we studied about the true righteousness that characterizes a child of God. We saw that the righteousness of the Pharisees was insincere, hypocritical and self centered. They practiced their religion for the applause of men, not for the desire to please God. In this lesson we will see true righteousness applied in the everyday activities of life. In Matthew chapter 6 we see several different areas of life that test whether a person is sincerely desiring to please God or seeking the approval and praise of other people.

In Matthew 6:1-18 Jesus addressed three areas in the Christian life: giving, praying and fasting. He followed the same four point outline for all three areas.
1. A warning not to do these things for the praise of men.
2. An assurance that those who seek the praise of men will get only the earthly reward of man's approval.
3. A command to give, pray and fast in private.
4. A promise that God, who sees in secret, will reward us openly.

Read Matthew 6:1-4 and notice the four points of the outline.

1._____

2._____

3._____

4._____

Giving to the poor, praying and fasting were important disciplines in the Jewish religion. Jesus certainly approved of these practices. In fact, he assumed that

IT IS POSSIBLE TO DO THE RIGHT THING WITH THE WRONG MOTIVE!

people would give, pray and fast, but he cautioned people to be sure their hearts were right as they practiced these different parts of religion.

Can you name any local organizations that publish donor lists? Are donors categorized according to the size of their contributions? These lists can appeal to man's desire for recognition. Jesus said giving to be noticed was like announcing one's gifts "with trumpets." Some might call this "tooting your own horn."

> The following is taken from *The Daily Bread*, December 28, 1998, entitled Secret Service written by David C. Egner. "When we serve God in secret, we receive a double reward. Not only will God one day reward us 'openly', but we will enjoy the memory of what we did." Thomas LaMance wrote: "Several years back...I was lounging around in the living room listening to the radio when my dad came in from shoveling snow. He looked at me and said, 'In 24 hours you won't even remember what you were listening to now. How about doing something for the next 20 minutes that you'll remember the next twenty years? I promise that you'll enjoy it every time you think of it.' 'What is it?' I asked. 'Well, son, there are several inches of snow on Mrs. Brown's walk,' he replied. 'Why don't you go see if you can shovel it off and get back home without her knowing you did it?' I did the walk in about 15 minutes. She never knew who did the job, and my dad was right. It's been a lot more than 20 years, and I've enjoyed the memory every time I've thought about it."

How could you avoid this when it comes to giving?

Jesus talked about giving to be seen by men. Next, he talked about praying to be seen and heard by men.

Read Matthew 6:5-6

Jesus gave us four guidelines for effective prayer in this passage:

Guideline 1: Part of our prayer must be in secret. Public prayer is just the tip of the iceberg. Our private prayer life should be much deeper and more intimate than our public prayer life.

Guideline 2: We must pray sincerely, without hypocrisy, not to be heard by men but to speak to God.

We read about a particular kind of insincere prayer in Matthew 6:7. What does it tell us?

_____

_____

_____

It is possible to treat what we call The Lord's Prayer this way—just recite the familiar words without thinking about them. Jesus didn't give us this prayer to be memorized and then recited over and over. He gave us this prayer to help us think about what we are praying, to keep us from using vain repetitions. He didn't tell us to pray in these specific words. He said, "This, then, is how you should pray." This prayer is designed as a pattern for our prayers. It could be called the "Model Prayer" since we should pray according to it.

Read Matthew 6:8

Why do we ask God for things if He already knows what we need?

Read James 4:2b

In the Lord's Prayer, our Model Prayer, notice that there are no singular pronouns. They are all plural. It begins with **our** Father. We are part of God's worldwide family of believers. You shouldn't be thinking "Lord bless Dad, Mom, brother and me, us four and no more." It is really a privilege and a joy to be an intercessor for other members of the family of believers. How exciting it is when you see God answer a prayer you have prayed on someone's behalf. Prayer is a "family affair." We are just children addressing our Father. How wonderful that we as believers can choose at any time to enjoy a conversation and fellowship with the King of Kings!

> In Alexander Solzhenitsyn's book, A Day in the Life of Ivan Denisovich, "Ivan endures all the horrors of a Soviet prison camp. One day he is praying with his eyes closed when a fellow prisoner notices him and says with ridicule, 'Prayers won't help you get out of here any faster.' Opening his eyes, Ivan answers, 'I do not pray to get out of prison but to do the will of God.'"

Guideline 3: We must pray for God's will. Matthew 6:9b-10

It is proper to put God's concerns first and then bring him our needs. The Lord's Prayer does not begin, "Our Father, give me." Prayer should be more than a wish list or a "to do" list we present to God.

It pleases God for us to ask him to meet our needs. He has designed prayer to be the way through which these needs are met. So we pray the equivalent of "Give us our daily bread." We should do more than pray generic, all encompassing prayers, like "Please bless everybody in the whole world." God likes us to be very specific about our needs so we can clearly see when he has given us a very specific answer.

"Bread" represents the necessities of life, not the luxuries. We probably need a lot less than we want. God gives us a promise in Philippians 4:19: "And my God will meet all your needs according to his glorious riches in Christ Jesus."

Guideline 4: We must pray with a forgiving spirit toward others. So we should pray the equivalent of verse 12 which says:

Matthew 6:14-15 is very plain about forgiveness also. It says:

So, if we want to be forgiven, we must forgive others! We will never have to forgive others as much as God has forgiven us.

Now look back at verse 13. It may seem like a strange request, "and lead us not into temptation, but deliver us from the evil one," or "from evil." We know that God will never tempt us to do evil. We realize our own weakness against the enemy, and we wisely pray that God will deliver us from yielding to Satan's advances.

The Lord's Prayer begins and ends with praise. It acknowledges the greatness of God. Some versions begin and end with, "Hallowed be thy name" and "for thine is the kingdom and the power and the glory, forever." Praise and thanksgiving are very important parts of our prayers. Do you praise and thank God often?

LESSON 11

THE LOVE CHAPTER

"And now these three remain: faith, hope and love. But the greatest of these is love" 1 Corinthians 13:13

1 Corinthians 13:1-13

This familiar passage is often used at weddings. It can be lifted out of Scripture and stand beautifully on its own. This chapter could be described as Paul's finest work. Every time I read these beautiful words my heart is moved. This amazing passage motivates me to put aside my fleshly desires. I long to love in the way my heavenly Father does. I always seem to fall so short of the mark, even though I desire his perfection.

Paul was actually using this writing to try to unify the church in Corinth. In some of the earlier chapters, Paul was stressing unity by urging them to love. Flip back through the first twelve chapters of the book of Corinthians and cite examples of this.

In 1 Corinthians 12, the previous chapter, Paul was writing about spiritual gifts and trying to correct some of the abuses of these gifts. (See 1 Corinthians 12:31)

Read 1 Corinthians 13:1

Paul was saying that if he could speak in every language of men and even the heavenly language of angels but didn't have love, he would only be *making noise.* He compared the noise to that of a gong or a clashing cymbal, which were commonly used in pagan ritual dances for heathen gods. They made plenty of noise but no melody.

Read 1 Corinthians 13:2

Who might this remind you of in our earlier studies?

Paul turned from knowledge and deeds of power in verse 2 to deeds of mercy and dedication in verse 3.

Read 1 Corinthians 13:3

These are extreme acts of selflessness but would still profit a person nothing without love.

What are three characteristics of love that show why it is so important in ministry?

L ove is _enriching._ Verses 1-3 show us that a ministry without love is worth absolutely nothing, but with love the ministry enriches the whole church. In fact, love enriches all it touches.

L ove is _edifying._ Look at 1 Corinthians 8:1b *"Knowledge puffs up, but love builds up."* Verses in 1 Corinthians 13:4-7 show us how love builds others up! It is love applied. *Read these.*

L ove is _enduring._ What love produces, lasts. It will be gold, silver and precious stones rather than wood, hay and stubble. When gifts are exercised with love, they become productive, effective and fruitful.

Read 1 Corinthians 13:8

There are different opinions today in the body of Christ as to when the sign gifts, such as tongues, prophecy in the sense of foretelling, healing, and miracles pass away. Some believe that God used these gifts in the early church and before Scripture was written, and they are no longer needed or valid today. Others believe that these gifts are to be used today and until Christ comes again, which will then make them obsolete.

Paul gave some analogies concerning what will happen when Christ returns, or when we die and go to heaven, if that happens before his return.

Read 1 Corinthians 13:9-11

Our knowledge will one day be complete. Paul exercised his maturity with determination. Childish things don't just pass away. The verb which Paul used indicates his determination not to be ruled by childish attitudes. It is in the perfect tense, which indicates that Paul put these things away with decision and finality.

The next analogy used was seeing through a poor mirror. What do you think mirrors were like in Paul's time? They were probably made of polished metal and the images weren't very clear. In this life, our view is dim and distorted, but one day we will see with perfect clarity.

Have you thought of a list of questions that you would like to ask God when you get to heaven?

Read 1 Corinthians 13:13

Faith, hope and love are the supreme virtues, but the greatest is love, partially because of its endurance. When we get to heaven, faith will be replaced by

_____, and hope will be replaced by _____, but

love will control _____.

Let's go back and re-read this passage. Insert Jesus where you see the word love and see how perfectly it fits. Now insert your name in verses 4 through 7. Sound funny? We have a long way to go but a wonderful goal.

If I speak in the tongues of men or of angels, but do not have _____, I am only a resounding gong or a clanging cymbal.

If I have the gift of prophecy and can fathom all mysteries and all knowledge, and if I have a faith that can move mountains, but do not have _____, I am nothing.

If I give all I possess to the poor and give over my body to hardship that I may boast, but do not have _____, I gain nothing.

_____ is patient, _____ is kind. It does not envy, it does not boast, it is not proud.

It does not dishonor others, it is not self-seeking, it is not easily angered, it keeps no record of wrongs.

_____ does not delight in evil but rejoices with the truth.

It always protects, always trusts, always hopes, always perseveres.

_____ never fails. But where there are prophecies, they will cease; where there are tongues, they will be stilled; where there is knowledge, it will pass away.

For we know in part and we prophesy in part, but when completeness comes, what is in part disappears.

When I was a child, I talked like a child, I thought like a child, I reasoned like a child.

When I became a man, I put the ways of childhood behind me.

For now we see only a reflection as in a mirror; then we shall see face to face. Now I know in part; then I shall know fully, even as I am fully known.

And now these three remain: faith, hope and _____. But the greatest of these is _____.

SPIRITUAL GIFTS

Read 1 Corinthians 12:1-11.

Each believer has at least one spiritual gift and many have more than one! Every person must function in other areas as well as those in which they are gifted. All Christians are expected to give, to witness, to offer hospitality to others, to show mercy to those in need, etc. God won't let us get away with saying we aren't going to do something because it is not our gift. People will tend to enjoy functioning in the areas of their gifts more than in other areas and will be more efficient and effective in those areas. So our primary ministry should be in the area where we are especially gifted to serve!

Have you ever noticed that you are just more "comfortable" in certain roles of work and service? Have you ever been frustrated or even jealous that you are not "better" in different areas?

The Bible gives us two warnings about gifts:

1 Corinthians 12:1

1 Timothy 4:14

Sometimes you have to try out different forms of service to discover your gift, or gifts. Once discovered, you should develop your gift, which is hard work.

There are different opinions on what are, and are not, spiritual gifts. Some people consider such things as music, art and prayer as spiritual gifts.

If we each made a list of our interpretation of what the Bible offers as "gifts", our lists would probably be a little different.

SPIRITUAL GIFTS

Support Gifts	Service Gifts	Sign Gifts
Apostleship	Administration	Miracles
Prophecy	Exhortation	Healing
Evangelism	Faith	Tongues
Pastor—Teacher	Giving	Interpretation of Tongues
Teaching	Helping	
Discerning Spirits	Showing Mercy	
	Hospitality	

The **Support Gifts** are the gifts that support the body of believers like bones support the human body. They have several characteristics in common:

- People with Support Gifts usually exercise these gifts to a group of people.
- Support Gifts have to do with communicating Scripture.
- These gifts help equip the saints for service.

The **Service Gifts** are the gifts that build up and encourage and strengthen the body of believers just like muscles in the human body.

- They are generally exercised away from the limelight or behind the scenes.
- They focus on other people.

The **Sign Gifts** are given to honor and praise God. Different denominations and individuals feel differently about "if and how" these gifts are used today.

1 Corinthians 12:7 emphasizes that the spiritual gifts are given for _____ of the body. The human body is better off when all areas are exercised. Since God has given each of us gifts, he has a ministry for us in the exercising of these gifts.

Let's look at the gifts and see if we can zero in on the characteristics and pick your gift out! You may also be able to pick out gifts of people you know well and perhaps understand them better.

Your gifts should be things you most enjoy doing. You should be the most efficient and the most effective in these areas. Your function in your gifts should flow easily and produce satisfaction. While hard work may be involved, the exercising of your gifts is not so much a chore as a joy and a pleasure. You have probably been asked by others to function in the area of your spiritual gifts because they recognize your ability there!

APOSTLESHIP

Generally speaking, an apostle is one who is sent forth, and in that sense we would qualify; but, technically speaking, these were the original twelve apostles of Christ.

- They had witnessed the resurrected Christ.
- Their ministries were authenticated by miracles and signs.
- Their word was authoritative.
- They were the founders of the early church and writers of much of the New Testament.

PROPHECY

In the years before the establishment of the New Testament church, the prophets brought a word directly from God. They would tell of a new revelation or foretell a future event. Prophecy means not only "fore tell" but also "forth tell" --tell forth the gospel message. It is the proclamation of the word of God in the wisdom and power of the Holy Spirit. In this sense, it continues as a gift in the church today.

TEACHING

Teaching is the ability to communicate Scriptural truth with accuracy, clarity, wisdom and simplicity. A gifted teacher makes what the Bible says clear. A teacher is a guardian of the truth. He doesn't usually originate anything new but defines, describes and declares existing revelation.

PASTOR–TEACHER

While the teacher guards the truth, the pastor guards the flock. He nourishes and protects the people in it, encouraging them and ministering to them with sensitivity to their particular needs.

FAITH

This isn't the kind of faith that brings us to salvation. All Christians have that. This is the ability to trust God without doubt or disturbance regardless of circumstances. People of faith aren't surprised when God answers prayers. These people are good cheer leaders and encouragers to others.

GIVING

We are certainly all expected to give, but the person with the gift of giving is sensitive to the needs of others and provides for them with great joy and generosity. People with the gift of giving often live modestly, spending minimum amounts on themselves because they prefer to give to others. Sometimes the ability to make money may accompany the gift of giving, but people do not have to be wealthy to exercise this gift. Remember the "giving widow" in the Bible. What did she give to the temple?

HELPING OR SERVING

This is the ability to assist and support others in the family of God in practical ways with great faithfulness and delight. These people tend to stay in the background but are essential to leaders.

EXHORTATION

This word can mean to encourage, urge, advise, and even to caution. This is what mothers do to get their kids to shape up! Exhorters are anxious to see other people live up to their potential. These people make good counselors.

EVANGELISM

These people have a burning desire to see people come to Christ. Everywhere they go they are sharing the gospel and seeing people become Christians. Can you think of any examples?

DISCERNMENT

This is the ability to distinguish right from wrong, good from evil, true from false, real from counterfeit.

HOSPITALITY

This person opens her home to others and sees to it that they feel at ease and welcome.

SHOWING MERCY

This is a compassionate person. Such people have the ability to empathize with the needs, pains, heartaches, disappointments and sorrows of others and to be an agent of healing and comfort. These people are good at visiting the sick, at helping the down and out, and organizing programs to meet the needs of others. Can you think of any examples?

ADMINISTRATION

This person is visionary, goal-oriented, decisive, calm, clear thinking and practical. The administrator has the ability to preside, govern, plan and organize with wisdom, fairness, kindness and efficiency. These people specialize in details and logistics.

SPIRITUAL GIFTS SKIT

This skit will show us some examples of these spiritual gifts in action. Seven women have gone to visit their friend, Cindy Sickly. Each of the women has a different spiritual gift and responds to the illness of the friend in a way characteristic of her gift.

MARY MERCY: (brings a pillow), I'm so sorry you haven't been feeling well. Here, let me put this pillow behind your back. Can I close the curtain so the sun doesn't get in your eyes?

HANNAH HELPER: (hands Cindy Sickly a magazine), I brought you a magazine. While I'm here, I can call and get your assignments and feed the dog. How about I cook you some dinner also?

CINDY SICKLY: Thanks for the help Hannah, but do you know how to cook?

HELEN HOSPITALITY: (Brings the flowers) I brought you some flowers from my garden to put by your bed. Would you like me to watch the door to see if any other visitors arrive? I can entertain them if you don't feel up to company.

GRACIE GIVING: I heard that your dad's out of work. I have taken up a collection. I hope this will help cover the costs. (She hands an envelope with money to Cindy.)

TERRI TEACHER: (Thumbing through her book) I have been looking up your symptoms in my medical book. I think I see the problem and can explain the different treatments.

FRANCES FAITH: I just know Cindy will be well in no time at all! I have been praying for her. She will be up and around in just a day or two; I am sure of it.

ANNIE ADMINISTRATOR: I have talked to your teachers and have all your assignments ready to pick up. I have notified the senior class committee that you will not be at the meeting tomorrow but arranged to have a report emailed to you. Do you have anything else pressing?

CINDY SICKLY: Meeting tomorrow? What meeting?

HELEN HOSPITALITY: We were to meet at the gym but I have changed the meeting to my house tomorrow to discuss prom decorations. I've already ordered pizza and baked brownies. I even invited the new girl to join us since she doesn't know many people.

MARY MERCY: Oh, I'm so glad. I remember just how lonesome I was when I first came to town. I can't wait to meet her and help her get to know everyone so she won't feel so lonely.

ANNIE ADMINISTRATOR: I'll make sure everyone knows it's at Helen's house now. I've already talked to our class president, and she has an agenda ready.

GRACIE GIVING: I have made a small donation toward the prom and will be collecting more money. I want us to get a good band and have really great decorations this year.

FRANCES FAITH: I just know it will be over the top!

HANNA HELPER: I can bring some folding chairs to the meeting. I think we will have a crowd.

TERRI TEACHER: I have looked over the agenda myself and it looks like everything is included to make the meeting a success. Cindy, you just read your magazine and rest. Don't worry about anything.

ALL: Hope you feel better soon. Bye.

LESSON 13

DAVID'S CONFESSION
Psalm 32 and 51

Our lesson today has great significance for each of us. What should we do when we sin? How can we avoid sin? How can we be forgiven and restored to fellowship with God?

How would you define sin?

How do you feel when you know you have sinned?

Nathan, the prophet, was sent by God to confront David. Read 2 Samuel 12:1-13. How would you like Nathan's job? Do you think God might use you at some time to help another person see his sin and get rid of it?

David wrote Psalm 32 and 51 in connection with his adultery with Bathsheba and the murder of her husband Uriah. These psalms give us insight into David's response to being confronted with his sins. After the confrontation, David turned to God in sincere repentance. He told Nathan, "I have sinned against the Lord." How might some people respond when confronted with their sin?

David poured out in detail his confession of guilt and request for forgiveness in Psalm 51:1-3.

> "Have mercy on me, O God, according to your unfailing love; according to your great compassion blot out my transgressions. Wash away all my iniquity and cleanse me from my sin. For I know my transgressions, and my sin is always before me."
>
> —King David

In this passage, David used three words for sin:

- _____, something perverse and crooked.

- _____, deliberate rebellion against God's will.

- _____, failing to measure up to God's standard of perfection.

David did not blame others for his sin. He took responsibility when he said, "my iniquity", "my sin" and "my transgressions." David asked God to wash away, cleanse, and blot out his sins, to clean him thoroughly and remove his sins from the record.

Read Psalm 51:1-2. What **three** aspects of God's forgiveness do you find in these verses?

Read Psalm 51:4

Other people are hurt by our sins, but it is God's law we break when we sin, and all sin is ultimately against him.

Read Psalm 51:5

Who's been around a baby lately? How do babies act? They cry when they want something! Everything is on their time table. Do you know people who continue to act that way past the infant stage?

God looks at our heart. People look at actions that stem from what is in our heart!

Read Psalm 51:7

David's confession continued. Hyssop was the little shrub the Jews used to put blood on the doorposts at the first Passover in Egypt. David's reference to cleansing with hyssop reminds us that it is the blood of Jesus Christ which cleanses us from all sin.

Read Psalm 51:8-12

God will always hear a sincere prayer of confession and answer it with forgiveness and restoration.

There are many sad consequences when a believer sins, but one of the worst is the loss of fellowship with God. You can observe David's deep anguish over his broken fellowship with God. David remembered what happened to King Saul, that God had taken his Spirit away from Saul and given it to David. So David prayed in Psalm 52:11 "Do not cast me from your presence or take your Holy Spirit from me." God does not remove his Holy Spirit from sinning believers today. When the Holy Spirit enters a believer at salvation, he never leaves him. David had not lost his salvation, but had lost the joy of his salvation. What did he ask God to do in Psalm 52:12?

Psalm 130:7b

"**...with the Lord is unfailing love and with Him is full redemption.**"

The difference between fellowship and relationship

Your relationship with your parents is parent-child. No matter what you do, you will always belong to your parents. Sometimes you may quarrel with your father or mother, and your fellowship with one of them is broken. Once we accept Christ we belong to God and will always have a relationship with him, but sin can break our fellowship with him.

Read Psalm 32:3-4. David told us how he felt before he confessed his sin and was forgiven.

Read Psalm 32:1-2, 5 for the **good news**!

For the believer in Christ, who has no unconfessed sin in her life and is walking in fellowship with God, there are many benefits of the Christian life, and we see some of those in Psalm 3 and 32.

- *We have a clean slate and a new beginning.*
- *Our joy returns.*
- *We experience the fruit of the spirit. (Galatians 5:22-23)*
- *We can pray to God and he will hear us. (Psalm 32:6a)*
- *God will protect and deliver us. (Psalm 32:6b-7)*
- *He will direct our path. (Proverbs 3:5-6)*
- *He will instruct us. (Proverbs 3:8)*
- *He surrounds us with his love. (Psalm 32:10)*

Hopefully our responses to God's goodness and mercy and forgiveness will parallel those of the psalmist David. He promised to tell others what God had done for him.

Psalm 51:13-15 says:

ILLUSTRATION

Illustration: Think of the biggest zit you have ever had. Remember how sore, red and swollen it was. What a relief it was when you popped it and all the nasty infection came out and the swelling went down. What a relief when we **allow** God to "pop" our hearts and squeeze out the sin and clean out the guilt.

There are three ways we can deal with sin, and these three ways have very different outcomes.

1. We can cover up our sins, practicing deceit and lying about them. When we do this, we lose God's fellowship.

2. We can confess our sins. Confession brings relief, freedom, forgiveness and a new beginning.

3. We can conquer our sins by yielding continually to the power of the Holy Spirit within us.

SEPARATED, SATURATED, SITUATED
Psalm One

The name "Psalms" comes from the Septuagint (the Greek translation of the Old Testament) where it originally referred to stringed instruments such as the harp and lyre, and later it referred to the songs that were accompanied by these instruments. The traditional Hebrew title means "praises", even though many of the psalms are actually prayers.

The Psalms were written as songs and were the hymnal for the Israelites. Their compilation probably spanned several centuries.

The Psalms were written in the form of poetry, although they do not rhyme nor do they have a standard meter like our poems today. The Psalms fall into several general categories:

- Hymns of praise (For God's majesty and attributes)
- Enthronement psalms (These celebrate the Lord as King over the nations and over the whole world.)
- Laments (Here individuals are asking deliverance from sickness or from their enemies. Some laments were sung by a nation in times of crisis or distress.)
- Thanksgiving (These psalms are to thank God for answered prayer and praise him for his saving help.)
- Royal psalms (These were sung for or by the present king.)
- Confessions of confidence in the Lord, often in spite of seemingly bleak circumstances
- Songs of Zion (These focus on the Holy City, Jerusalem, and the worship in the temple there.)
- Liturgical (These psalms were used primarily in public worship.)
- Messianic (These psalms foreshadow the coming of Jesus Christ and his work on the cross.)
- Instructional psalms (These tell us how to live.)
- Wisdom psalms (These reflect on the meaning of life and the wisdom of God.)

Psalm 1 is called a wisdom psalm and it presents two opposite ways to live. This kind of presentation is seen in different ways throughout Scripture. Some examples are as follows:

• Galatians 6:7-8

• Matthew 7:24-27

• Matthew 7:13-14

With God or Without God?

There are two ways to live—with God or without God, as righteous people or as wicked. Psalm 1 makes this dichotomy very clear. It tells us that either we are blessed or we are perishing. Read Psalm 1.

God wants to bless his people! He wants us to be recipients and channels of blessing, but he has given us certain conditions for receiving blessings. God enjoys blessing your life, but you must be "blessable." Certainly, we desire and delight in being blessed by God. What does it take for us to be in a position to receive God's blessing?

We must be **separated from the world.** The world is anything that separates us from God or causes us to disobey him. Separation is not isolation but contact without contamination.

Psalm 1:1

Being blessed involves having discernment and avoiding the steps that lead to sin. Sin is usually a gradual process. Notice the gradual decline of the sinner in verse 1.

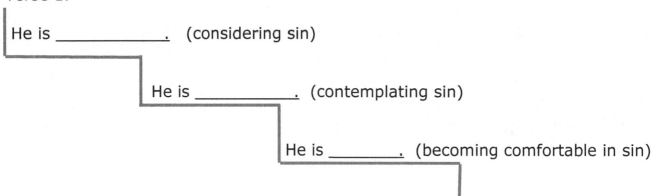

He is _____. (considering sin)

He is _____. (contemplating sin)

He is _____. (becoming comfortable in sin)

Becoming worldly is *progressive*. It happens by degrees. We make friends with the world; we become spotted by the world; we love the world, become conformed to it and end up condemned with it. Lot is an example of someone who became worldly. He looked toward Sodom, pitched his tent toward Sodom and then moved into Sodom. As a result, he lost everything.

To be blessed, we must not only be separated from the world but we must also be **saturated with the Word**. What you delight in will direct your life, so be careful what you enjoy.

Psalm 1:2

He delights so much in God's word that he *meditates* on it day and night. We saturate ourselves with the Word by meditating on it. Meditation is to the spirit what digestion is to the body. When we meditate on the Word, we allow the Spirit of God within us to "digest" the Word of God for us. So, not only do we delight in the Word, it becomes a source of spiritual nourishment for us. One dictionary defines "meditation" as "to think in view of doing." We can study our Bible to get information but then we need to "meditate" on how to relate it to our life. We study to serve; we meditate to live. Study can bring growth to our mind, but meditation brings growth to our inner being.

Psalm 1:3

A tree is a blessing. It holds soil, provides shade and homes for birds and squirrels, and produces fruit. The godly are like trees, with root systems that go deep into the spiritual resources of God's grace. But, sadly, many professing Christians are not like trees but like artificial plants that look like the real thing but are not. Others are like cut flowers with no roots. They may be beautiful for a while, but they will eventually die.

A tree must have roots to live. The question we need to ask ourselves is, "Where are our roots?" The most important part of our lives is our root system. It determines our nourishment, and it also determines our stability and strength when the storms come and the winds blow.

"When we plant a tree, we select the spot where we want it and the type of tree best suited for that location and for the purpose we had in mind. God knows where He wants to plant us, and He has a purpose in planting us there. It may not be the place of our choice, but it is the place of His choosing." Millie Stamm, *Meditation Moments,* (Zondervan Publishing Corporation, 1967 P. 70)

We only bear fruit when we have roots, and we must draw upon spiritual resources to bring forth fruit in due season. *Where* we place our roots is of paramount importance. The person God can bless is **situated by the waters**.

We must be:

Separated from the world.

Saturated with the Word.

Situated by the waters.

Only as we grow our roots deeply into the spiritual resources of God's grace will we produce fruit.

Read Psalm 1:4

We must be careful not to be like Christians who are dry and withered and depend upon their own resources. They are like "chaff" which has no roots, produces no fruit, and is blown about by any wind of doctrine.

Read Psalm 1:5-6

Contrast a tree and chaff and you will see the difference between the godly and the ungodly. The godly receive blessing but the ungodly receive judgment. The ungodly reject the Word of God and will perish without hope. How tragic that anyone is perishing when Jesus offers abundant life! The psalm starts with "blessed" and ends with "perish." The choice is ours.

Read Psalm 92:12-14 for a beautiful parallel passage.

WHAT IS CHAFF?

Chaff is:

LESSON 15

HOW DO I LIVE THE CHRISTIAN LIFE?

How did you enter the Christian life?

How can you live the Christian life?

Read Galatians 3:3

It is crucial to know how to enter the Christian life, but it is also important to know how to live it once you have entered it. The issue of how the Christian life is to be lived can be settled by answering one key question: how did you enter the Christian life? Did you receive the Holy Spirit by the works of the law or by faith?

How a person begins determines how he ends. The Christian life is of one nature. It doesn't change midstream. A cow is always a cow. A calf doesn't grow up to be a horse. It would be foolish to believe that the Christian life is of one nature at its beginning but that it changes its nature as it goes along. A person lives the Christian life the same way he entered the Christian life—by faith from start to finish.

Mary Love Eyster shares, "I was so foolish and ignorant for 30 years. I believed that old adage that 'God helps those who help themselves.' I thought the way to live the Christian life was to do my best and only ask God for help when I couldn't handle things. I thought the less often I had to bother God for help, the more pleased He would be with me. I had a spiritual beginning, because that's the only way to enter the Christian life, but I was trying to live for God in my own strength and wisdom. I felt I was unsuccessful because I hadn't tried hard enough yet, and I kept pushing to try to do better."

Some believers choose bondage rather than liberty!   Some people call this **legalism.**   Look this word up.   What is there about legalism that would lure a Christian into turning from grace to law?

Legalism appeals to the flesh.   The flesh loves to be religious and to obey laws, to observe holy occasions, even to fast, so it can boast about its religious achievements.   There is nothing wrong with these activities if the attitude is right, but in legalism these things are done to glorify the person rather than God.

Legalism also appeals to the senses.   The legalists do not want to worship God in spirit nor walk by faith.   They want to walk by sight and by other senses as well. People who depend upon legalism can measure themselves and compare themselves with **others.**   We should always use Jesus as our standard of measure.   Even on the cross he said, "Father, forgive them."

Guilt is a primary tactic of legalists as they try to take away the joy we have in our freedom in Christ.   Legalists are also experts at **intimidation**.   They can give you a disapproving stare or point a finger your way.

It is very important to read our Bibles, attend Sunday school, pray and witness. These things are the backbone of the Christian life, but they can be done in such a mechanical way that they prove to be ineffective. It is more important to meet with Jesus when we pray than just log in so many minutes of quiet time.   We want to apply what we are reading in God's word rather than just reading so many verses.   We also want to allow the Holy Spirit to do his thing in our lives instead of just following the lives of other Christians (including your parents).

Keep our eyes on him and not each other!

"You're not the boss of me!"

My grandchildren like to tell each other, "You're not the boss of me." The matter of the Holy Spirit is like this: will you take charge of your own life or will you allow the Holy Spirit to work in and through your yielded life?   **And be the boss of you!**

Would you like to have the Holy Spirit living the Christian life through your body today? WHO IS THE HOLY SPIRIT?

In John chapters 14, 15 and 16, Jesus referred to the Holy Spirit as "He", not it. Throughout the Bible, we see that the Holy Spirit is God Himself.   What are the following attributes of the Holy Spirit?

Hebrews 9:14

Luke 1:35

Psalm 139:7

1 Corinthians 2:10-11

Read John 14:16-17, John 15:26-27, John 14:26 and John 16:12-15 to discover more. Record your findings below.

The Holy Spirit is Part of the Trinity

The first mention of the Holy Spirit is in Genesis 1:2. See also Genesis 1:26. The Holy Spirit is an active part of the Trinity. He is the spirit of the Father (Matthew 10:20) and the spirit of his Son (Galatians 4:6). In John 15:26 we find all three persons of the Godhead (Trinity) mentioned.

Promise of the Holy Spirit

Old Testament

1 Samuel 16:13

Exodus 31:3

New Testament

Luke 1:35

John 16:7

John 14:16

John 1:8

At Pentecost

Acts 2:14-17

Next to the importance of Christ's coming to earth is the coming of the Holy Spirit.

Have you ever tried to operate something electrical and finally found out that the reason it wasn't working was because you had forgotten to plug it in? Don't you imagine that the angels watch us and are astounded by our efforts to make life work without plugging into God's power? I am amazed at myself when I forget that the infinite, personal Spirit of Christ lives within me to guide my life and give me power. His Spirit enables me to do God's will, to show God's attitudes, and to fulfill God's purposes. But I have to stay plugged in through prayer, reflection on God's word, and complete reliance on his power—not my own!

LESSON 16

SHARING MY FAITH

"Therefore go and make disciples of all nations, baptizing them in the name of the Father and of the Son and of the Holy Spirit, and teaching them to obey everything I have commanded you. And surely I am with you always, to the very end of the age." Matthew 28:19-20

In Lesson 12, we discussed spiritual gifts, and one of those was evangelism. We described evangelism as a "burning desire" to see lost people introduced to Christ. Even though we do not all have a "calling" to evangelism, we are all instructed to carry out the great commission of Christ given to us in the Matthew 28 passage.

Do you find it hard to share your faith? Why do you think this is so?

Who would love to silence you?

Why is it important, even crucial, that we share our faith with others?

Undoubtedly, someone shared the story of Christ's love with you. What difference did it make in your life? What difference could it make in someone else's life? What are you waiting on?

MY TESTIMONY

Ask God to guide you! (James 1:5)

A simple outline could be:

- My life before I accepted Christ.
- How I accepted Christ.
- My life after accepting Christ.

My life before Christ:

> You might tell of areas in your life that were "self centered" or in need of Christ's touch. Did you feel that something was "missing" in your life? Were you drawn to believers by their characteristics?   Always be truthful when sharing.

How I accepted Christ:

> Explain exactly how you received Christ. The person you are sharing with should be able to accept Christ by your clear example. Some people remember an exact time and place when they made their decision to trust Jesus Christ with their lives.   Some even celebrate their "spiritual birthdays." Others may have made their decision as children, knowing in their hearts there was a time they wanted Jesus controlling their lives but were unable to recall an exact date or time.

If you're not certain whether you have invited Jesus into your heart, you can make certain by asking him to be your Savior:

A—Admit you are a sinner and ask for forgiveness (Romans 3:23, 1 John 1:9);

B—Believe in Jesus as your Savior and become a child of God by receiving him (John 3:16, John 1:12);

C—Confess that Jesus is Lord and choose to follow him daily (Romans 10:9, Luke 9:23)!

My life after accepting Christ:

> How has your life been different? Do you have a strong desire to walk closely with God and to denounce sin? What about your prayer life?

It is important to write your testimony down and to practice sharing it. This will give you confidence because you will know what you are going to say and how you want to say it. You will want to avoid negativity, stereotyping and mentioning church denominations in your story.

You are not alone when you are sharing. Jesus promised that the Holy Spirit will give you power when you witness according to Acts 1:8. He also promised that your efforts will not be in vain according to Isaiah 55:11.

John 14:6 tells us that Jesus is the only way to God. People are hungry for him and need him in their lives. Your friends need forgiveness. Strangers you meet need to hear of God's love. A life controlled by God's love and producing much fruit is the best life that there is!

MY TESTIMONY

<u>Opening sentence, attention getter, or thought provoking question:</u>

<u>Before I became a Christian I lived and thought this way:</u>

<u>How I received Christ:</u>

<u>After I received Christ these changes took place:</u>

<u>Closing remarks (could share a favorite verse):</u>

LESSON 17

TESTIMONY SHARING

Ask God to speak through the power of the Holy Spirit as you share what he would want you to say. Be yourself and be truthful. If you are nervous, it's ok; that should be expected. (Remember who does not want you to learn to share!) Philippians 4:13, "I can do all things through Him who strengthens me."

Write the names of those in your group below and leave space for comments. Let them know what touched you most about their testimony and give advice on what they could improve.

LESSON 18

THE TWENTY THIRD PSALM

Read the 23rd Psalm.

David wrote this psalm. As you think back over his life, what do you think inspired him to write this beautiful psalm?

Let's examine each verse together. Read and record what you think the following verses mean.

Psalm 23:1

Remember where David began his incredible life, in the pastures, shepherding sheep. What are some of the needs of sheep?

How are we like sheep?

Isaiah 53:6

Don't we tend to stray into situations that get us into trouble? We allow problems and irritations to steal our joy and peace and disrupt our sleep. We are vulnerable to predators from both the natural world and the supernatural world.

Do we need a shepherd? Yes, indeed! Psalm 23 tells us that the Lord is our Shepherd. Psalm 100:3b says:

What does our Shepherd do for us?

Philippians 4:19

Psalm 23:2

What do you think the psalmist meant by "green pastures" and "quiet waters"?

What invitation is God giving us in John 7:37b?

How can we do that?

Have you ever heard of a cast sheep? Sheep have short legs and heavy bodies. Sometimes when they lie down, especially if there is an indentation in the ground, they will roll over in such a way that makes it impossible for them to get up without help.

Have you ever felt like a cast sheep?

Who has helped you up?

What can we do to help each other up?

Psalm 23:3

Why would our souls need restoring?

How does God restore our souls?

1 John 1:9

Matthew 11:28

Why would he lead us in paths of righteousness for his name's sake? How would you feel if you did something that caused your family shame? Would you want to do things that would bring shame or disgrace to the name of our Heavenly Father?

Our Good Shepherd defines for us the path of righteousness in the Bible. God's word tells us the things we should do and things we should not do. When we become Christians we get on the right path, but sometimes we stray from the path. Then we need to confess our sin and repent and ask God to put us back on the path of righteousness. Our Shepherd helps us stay on the right path.

Psalm 23:4

Once we have accepted Christ, the Holy Spirit comes to live within us and will never leave us. We will not take even one step in the valleys, the hard times, of life alone. Our Shepherd will be right there with us.

Matthew 28:20b gives us some reassuring words from Jesus. Write those words:

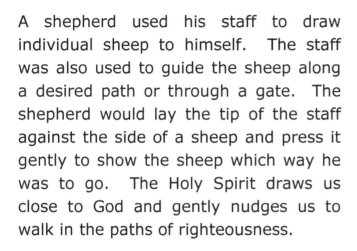

A shepherd used his staff to draw individual sheep to himself. The staff was also used to guide the sheep along a desired path or through a gate. The shepherd would lay the tip of the staff against the side of a sheep and press it gently to show the sheep which way he was to go. The Holy Spirit draws us close to God and gently nudges us to walk in the paths of righteousness.

The rod was the shepherd's weapon with which he protected both himself and his sheep. The shepherd also used his rod to correct wandering sheep, just as God's word corrects us when we stray away from obeying God.

Psalm 23:5

What do you think of when you hear the word table?

The anointing of oil has different purposes. Insects of all kinds can become annoying and upsetting to the sheep in the summer. The antidote is for the shepherd to rub the sheep's heads with a specially prepared oil mixture.

There are many aggravations and irritations that buzz around us, upsetting us and stealing our peace and joy. Just as oil is applied to the sheep, God's Holy Spirit must continually anoint us to counteract the frustrations of life and bring us peace and joy.

The antlers of the rams were greased so when they fought their horns would slide off each other rather than interlocking and causing injuries. The Holy Spirit will keep us from "locking horns" with other people and make us kinder and gentler in our relationships.

Another purpose of the oil was to heal wounds. The Holy Spirit comes alongside to comfort and heal us when we have been wounded by the unkindness of others or the trauma of tragic events.

What might an "overflowing cup" represent at the end of the verse?

Share how God has blessed you.

Psalm 23:6

It is easy to see that God's goodness and mercy are following us when all is going well in our lives. But when there are health problems, financial difficulties, divorces, tragic events, or the deaths of people we love, it is much harder to see God's goodness and mercy, but it is still there. It is not our circumstances that reveal how much God loves us – it is the cross! Never forget this: "Jesus loves me! This I know, for the Bible tells me so."

The place which God has prepared for those who love him will be beautiful and wonderful far beyond anything we can imagine. It will be a place of "no mores" – no more sickness, sorrow, pain, death, tears, or struggles. The best part is that God will live there with us and so will Jesus and our loved ones who die in Christ. No matter how hard our journey to heaven may be, the destination will be worth it all!

This week, take notice of the many ways your Shepherd, Jesus, is "providing and guiding" in your life.

LESSON 19

THE PROVERBS 31 WOMAN

Read Proverbs 31:10-31

Have you ever known someone who seemed to have it all together and made you feel intimidated? Have you looked at beautiful movie stars and felt inadequate? When you hear the description of the Proverbs 31 woman, how do you feel?

Some Bible scholars believe that the Proverbs 31 woman is a compilation of great womanly virtues rather than one single, specific woman. Whether she is one woman or many, she is the personification of wisdom. It is one thing to talk about virtues like wisdom, faith, integrity, courage, etc. in the abstract, but it is another thing to see these qualities lived out in a specific person, in other words, personified.

> Mark Twain once said, "Few things are harder to put up with than the annoyance of a good example."

If we want to see **faith** personified, we can look at the life of Abraham. Can you give an example of faith in Abraham's life?

If we want to see **integrity** personified, we can look at the life of Daniel. Can you give an example of integrity in Daniel's life?

If we want to see **courage** personified, we can look at the shepherd boy David. Can you give an example of courage in David's life?

If we want to see **evangelism** personified, we can look at Paul. He suffered so much for the spreading of the gospel, yet continued to preach. What did this eventually cost him?

If we want to see the personification of **wisdom**, we can find it in the Proverbs 31 woman. Let's look at her life and see how she lived out some of the qualities that are found in wise people.

Proverbs 31:10

A wife of noble character is worth more than _____. We might call her a jewel of a woman!

A good name is worth more than what?

Proverbs 22:1
A good name...

Proverbs 31:11-12

Her husband has full _____ in her! He knows he can trust her.

She brings him good not _____, all the days of her life.

What are some ways a woman can bring a man good and not harm?

The Proverbs 31 woman is not lazy at all.

Read Proverbs 31:13, 15, 17-18 and 27. Record a few of her accomplishments:

The Proverbs 31 woman is a woman of excellence. What she does, she does well and thoroughly. She doesn't settle for something just because it's easy, but goes for quality!

Proverbs 31:11, 12 and 29

DEFINE: NOBLE

You might say she is a woman of "integrity."

The following is a question asked in the book <u>The Day America Told the Truth</u>, written by James Patterson and Peter Kim, 1991.

"What are you willing to do for $10,000,000?" Two-thirds of Americans polled would agree to at least one, some to several, of the following:

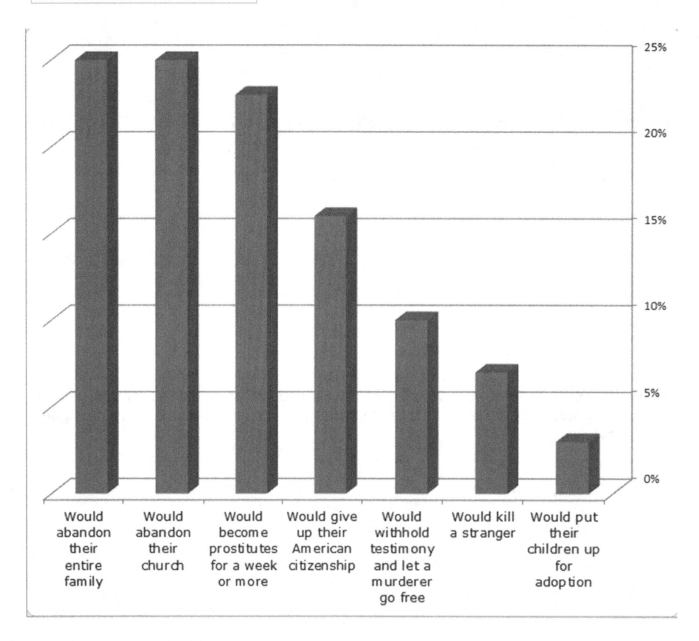

Would abandon their entire family	Would abandon their church	Would become prostitutes for a week or more	Would give up their American citizenship	Would withhold testimony and let a murderer go free	Would kill a stranger	Would put their children up for adoption

The woman we are talking about would not compromise her integrity at any price.

She takes care of things because she should, it is right and she loves her family, not because she is trying to impress others.

Her good character reflects well upon her husband.

Write Proverbs 31:23 and explain.

Have you ever heard the saying, "Behind every great man is a great woman?" Your influence on a man can be immense.

> "Behind every great man is a great woman."

The Proverbs 31 woman also trains her children up in the way in which they should go.

Proverbs 31:26.

Napoleon Bonaparte was quoted, "The future destiny of the child is always the work of the mother. Let France have good mothers, and she will have good sons." Have you ever heard the saying, "the hand that rocks the cradle is the hand that rules the world?"

The Jukes Family

In 1875 Richard L. Dugdale announced his study of the Jukes family in the annual report of the Prison Association of New York. His findings were later published in the Carnegie Institute of Washington by Arthur H. Estabrook. Max Jukes was an unbelieving man, and he married a woman of like character who lacked principle. Among his known descendants, over 1,200 were studied. Three hundred and ten became professional vagrants; 440 physically wrecked their lives by a debauched lifestyle; 130 were sent to prison for an average of 13 years each, 7 of them for murder. There were over 11 who became alcoholics; 60 became habitual thieves; 190 were public prostitutes. Of the 20 who learned a trade, 10 of them learned the trade in a state prison. They cost the state about $1,500,000 and they made no contribution whatever to society.

The Edwards Family

The following is taken from a 1925 reprint of Winship's report on the descendants of Jonathan Edwards. This was about the same era as Max Jukes. Jonathan Edwards was a man of God, and he married a woman of like character. Three hundred of their descendants became clergymen, missionaries, and theological professors; over 100 became college professors; over 100 became attorneys, 30 of them judges; 60 became authors of good classic books; 14 became presidents of universities. There were numerous giants in American industry who emerged from this family. Three became United States congressmen, and one became the vice president of the United States.

Do you think the way you raise your children is important?

Does it matter?

The Proverbs 31 woman is a good business woman.

Proverbs 31:16, 18a and 24. She makes the most of her financial opportunities.

Over and over in Proverbs we have been encouraged to be kind to the poor, and the wise Proverbs 31 woman does just that.

Proverbs 31:20

The Proverbs 31 woman plans ahead for the needs of her family.

Proverbs 31:21-22, 25

Discuss what this scripture means.

Proverbs 31:30

A woman's good character and virtue can grow stronger and more attractive as her youthful beauty fades. A wise woman spends her time and effort in cultivating these instead of trying to hold on too tightly to her physical beauty. What are some ways you can "grow" your character and virtue?

Remember Proverbs 1:7, "The fear of the Lord is the beginning of wisdom"? The Proverbs 31 woman was praised because she feared the Lord. This was her most important characteristic.

Proverbs 31:28, 31

The fear of the Lord was the secret of the staying power of the Proverbs 31 woman. She received the grace that his Spirit supplies. The greatest worth of the virtuous woman is her devotion to the Lord.

Jesus is the greatest example we will ever have, but who of us mortals could ever hope to achieve what Jesus achieved? By ourselves, the situation is absolutely hopeless.

Galatians 2:20a

2 Corinthians 4:7

There is no way we can live the Christian life, but we can experience it, because God loves us so much he is willing to live it in and through us through the wisdom and power of his Holy Spirit.

> The Proverbs 31 woman is not just a good example for us to try to copy. God didn't put her in the Bible to frustrate and discourage us. The Proverbs 31 woman is a picture of what God wants to do through us as women, if we allow his Holy Spirit to control us.

TEACHER'S GUIDE

*Page numbers in the Teacher's Guide, beginning with Lesson One (the next page), correlate with the page numbers in the Student's Guide at the beginning of this book.

LESSON 1

INTRODUCTION TO PROVERBS

"The fear of the Lord is the beginning of wisdom." Proverbs 1:7

Certain clothes go in and out of style. It is said that if you keep out of date clothes long enough, they will eventually come back in style. Amazingly enough, even bell bottoms have recycled! Certain words are like fashion; their use comes in and out of style. We use them for a while and then they are dropped from our vocabularies. They are considered outdated or old fashioned. One of my grandfather's favorite words was "wholesome." I don't hear that word used much anymore.   Another word I don't hear often is "wisdom." This is the key word in our study of Proverbs.

 **WIZBITS** We have a collection of wise sayings in our society today, sayings that have been passed down orally from generation to generation. Some are based on Scripture; others have come from literature; some have come from observation.   What WIZBITS can you recall? I'll get you started.

Two heads are better than <u>one</u>.

Actions speak louder than <u>words</u>.

All that glitters is not <u>gold</u>.

_____

_____

_____

Proverbs 1:1 ascribes its "wise words" to whom? <u>*Solomon*</u>_____

Most of the book of Proverbs is closely linked to Solomon. He was the son of King David and Bathsheba. He inherited the kingdom when his father David died.

Read I Kings 3:5-13. This passage of Scripture gives us important insight into Solomon's wisdom. God appeared to Solomon in a dream.   God instructed Solomon to ask for whatever he wanted, and it would be granted.

What would you ask for?

What did Solomon request?

Verse 9,   *"I ask that you give me an obedient heart so I can rule the people in the right way and will know the difference between right and wrong."* Solomon asked for wisdom to make the right decisions.

Just how much wisdom did God grant Solomon? I Kings 4:29, I Kings 4:32

God gave Solomon wisdom and very great insight; and a breadth of understanding as measureless as the sand on the seashore. He passed down some of his wisdom to us!

The book of Proverbs encourages EVERYONE to get wisdom.   Gaining wisdom should be a top priority for us--just as it was for Solomon.

Proverbs 2:2 *"Incline your ear to wisdom, and apply your heart to understanding."*

Proverbs 3:21 *"My son, preserve sound judgment and discernment, do not let them out of your sight."*

Proverbs 13:12   *"Apply your heart to instruction and your ears to words of knowledge."*

Wisdom was the number one priority for Solomon, and he tells everyone in Proverbs just how important wisdom is in life.

Proverbs 16:16 *"How much better to get wisdom than gold, to choose understanding rather than silver."*

Proverbs 3:13-15   *"Blessed is the man who finds wisdom, the man who gains understanding, for she is more profitable than silver and yields better returns than gold. She is more precious than rubies; nothing you desire can compare with her."*

Apparently, Solomon believed obtaining wisdom was of more importance than obtaining _wealth_.

Charles Swindoll said, "Foolish indeed is the person who considers himself safe and sound because he has money….Money, in the final analysis, brings no lasting satisfaction, certainly not in the area of things that really matter. There are many things that no amount of money can buy. Think of it this way:

Money can buy medicine, but not health.
Money can buy a house, but not a home.
Money can buy companionship, but not friends.
Money can buy food, but not an appetite.
Money can buy a bed, but not sleep.
Money can buy the good life, but not eternal life.

It is God alone who is able to supply us with all things to enjoy."

We are truly wealthy when we learn that the greatest gifts ever obtained are the ones that only God can give. What "treasures" might you gain in an obedient life to him?

See Galatians 5:22-23 "But the fruit of the Spirit is love, joy, peace, patience, kindness, goodness, faithfulness, gentleness and self-control. Against such things there is no law."

LESSON 2

THE BENEFITS OF WISDOM

"He who cherishes understanding prospers." Proverbs 19:8

In our last lesson, we learned that we are to incline our ears to wisdom, preserve sound judgment, and apply our hearts to instruction. We learned that it is better to have wisdom than wealth. Like Solomon, obtaining wisdom should be at the top of our list of desires.

In this lesson, we will look at the benefits of having Godly wisdom and the consequences of relying on human wisdom alone.

What benefits of having wisdom do the following verses convey to us?

Proverbs 3:16-18 *"Long life is in her right hand; in her left hand are riches and honor. Her ways are pleasant ways, and her paths are peace. She is a tree of life to those who embrace her; those who lay hold of her will be blessed."*

Proverbs 2:11-12 *"Discretion will protect you, and understanding will guard you. Wisdom will save you from the ways of wicked men, from men whose words are perverse."*

Proverbs 3:12 *"When you walk, your steps will not be hampered; when you run, you will not stumble."*

Proverbs 3:7b-8 *"Fear the Lord and shun evil. This will bring health to your body and nourishment to your bones."*

Proverbs 19:8b *"He who cherishes understanding prospers."*

Proverbs 24:5 *"A wise man has great power, and a man of knowledge increases strength."*

Proverbs 24:14 *"Know also that wisdom is sweet to your soul; if you find it, there is a future hope for you, and your hope will not be cut off."*

Proverbs 3:5-6 *"Trust in the Lord with all your heart and lean not on your own understanding; in all your ways acknowledge him, and he will make your paths straight."*

Solomon not only commented on the benefits of Godly wisdom, but he also discussed the consequences of folly and warned us over and over about the results of relying on human wisdom alone.   What are some of those results found in the following verses?

Proverbs 24:19-20 *"Do not fret because of evil men or be envious of the wicked, for the evil man has no future hope, and the lamp of the wicked will be snuffed out."*

Proverbs 5:22-23 *"The evil deeds of a wicked man ensnare him; the cords of sin hold him fast. He will die for lack of discipline, led astray by his own great folly."*

KEY TO SUCCESS

Each of you has already experienced or will encounter hardships and unfamiliar terrain in your life. The key to your success is learning to walk by faith and not by sight.

Many people flirt with temptation, believing they can rescue themselves at any time, but they wind up being caught in evil and suffering the consequences of their folly. Can you think of any examples?

There once was an eagle perched on a block of ice above Niagara Falls. The swift current was rapidly carrying the ice and its passenger close to the edge. Other birds warned the eagle of the danger ahead, but he replied, "I have great, powerful wings, and I can fly off my perch any time I please." When the edge of the falls was only a few feet away, the eagle spread his wings to mount up, only to discover that his claws had become frozen to the block of ice.

Where can I get this kind of great wisdom?

Proverbs 1:7 "*The fear of the Lord is the beginning of wisdom and discipline.*"

Proverbs 2:6 "*For the Lord gives wisdom, and from his mouth come knowledge and understanding.*"

James 1:5 "*If any of you lack wisdom, he should ask God, who gives generously to all without finding fault, and it will be given to him.*"

Psalm 111:10 "*Reverence for the Lord is the foundation of true wisdom. The rewards of wisdom come to all who obey him.*"

If we are going to walk by God's wisdom, we must have a **teachable spirit**. What do you think this means? *We must be willing to learn.*

Proverbs 9:7-9 "*Whoever corrects a mocker invites insult; whoever rebukes a wicked man incurs abuse. Do not rebuke a mocker or he will hate you; rebuke a wise man and he will love you. Instruct a wise man and he will add to his learning.*"

Proverbs 12:1 "*Whoever loves discipline loves knowledge, but he who hates correction is stupid.*"

Proverbs 12:15 "*The way of a fool seems right to him, but a wise man listens to advice.*"

There seems to be more advice out there than there are those who are seeking it! Have you seen restaurants or businesses that solicit your opinion with survey cards or even post 1-800 numbers for feedback? What eagerness they are showing to improve their products and serve the public better. What eagerness to listen, to learn, and to grow! Then I ask myself, do I have that kind of attitude toward God and others? Am I eager to provide better service to people in Christ's name, to have my weaknesses and faults pointed out so that I might grow? Am I ready to take criticism, suggestions, and advice? A teachable spirit and an eagerness to learn are marks of true wisdom. The next time that we feel so quick to defend ourselves when criticized, regardless of who is giving the advice, stop and pray, "Lord, are you giving me a bit of gentle advice that I need to hear?"

> **ROOM FOR IMPROVEMENT IS THE**
>
> **LARGEST ROOM IN THE WORLD**

You can have Godly wisdom if you choose to have an intimate relationship with his Son. Knowing him in a personal way is our direct path to the wisdom of God. We can choose to seek God's wisdom or we can rely on our own human ability— it's our choice. However, we will reap the consequences of our decision.

LESSON 3

PROVERBS – FAMILY LIFE

Family life is the topic of our lesson today. Solomon gave us some of his great wisdom for dealing with family situations. He specifically talked about husband-wife and parent-child relationships, but many of his principles can be applied to all kinds of family relationships.

Solomon emphasized faithfulness and purity in marriage for the men, warning several times not to become involved with adulteresses. His warning to be faithful to one's spouse in marriage could be written to women also, because faithfulness is basic in a successful and happy marriage.

Proverbs 27:8 *"Like a bird that strays from its nest is a man who strays from his home."*

Proverbs 6:27-29 *"Can a man scoop fire into his lap without his clothes being burned? Can a man walk on hot coals without his feet being scorched? So is he who sleeps with another man's wife; no one who touches her will go unpunished."*

Proverbs 5:15-18 *"Be faithful to your own wife, just as you drink water from your own well. Don't pour your water in the streets; don't give your love to just any woman. These things are yours alone and shouldn't be shared with strangers. Be happy with the wife you married when you were young. She gives you joy, as your fountain gives you water."*

Why is marriage hard and why do you feel so many marriages today do not last? *A great question for discussion. Interject Biblical truth. From the previous verse; he's not happy and she's not giving joy. These are signs of being a "taker" and not a "giver."*

My grandmother had a great statement, "I work on my marriage every day." Men and women change through the years. It takes effort to keep a marriage fresh! I have found that keeping a close walk with God helps more than anything else.

Psalm 127:1a *"Unless the Lord builds the house, its builders labor in vain..."*

Proverbs 14:1 *"The wise woman builds her house, but with her own hands the foolish one tears hers down."*

Proverbs 24:3-4 paints a beautiful picture of a harmonious marriage and family, *"By wisdom a house is built, and through understanding it is established; through knowledge its rooms are filled with rare and beautiful treasures."*

There are no treasures on earth more beautiful to me

than the members of my family.

Solomon had instructions for children also. Read the following verses and record their advice.

Proverbs 4:1 *"Listen, my sons, to the father's instruction; pay attention and gain understanding." Ask: Who should you listen to if your earthly father is giving bad advice? Your heavenly father.*

Proverbs 1:8-9 *"Listen, my son, to your father's instruction and do not forsake your mother's teaching. They will be a garland to grace your head and a chain to adorn your neck." Discuss: What could these symbols represent?*

Proverbs 3:1-2 *"My son, do not forget my teaching, but keep my commands in your heart, for they will prolong your life many years and bring you prosperity." Listening to your parents can actually make you live longer!*

At every age we can remember and profit from the things our parents have taught us.

Proverbs 19:27 *"Stop listening to instruction, my son, and you will stray from the words of knowledge."*

If children are to heed the instruction of parents, it goes without saying that parents must give their children wise instruction to remember. Other family members such as grandparents and aunts and uncles can contribute important instruction and impart wisdom as well. Would you like to tell of someone in your life who has shared his or her wisdom with you?

Satan would love nothing more than to destroy homes. He would delight in having everyone looking out for his or her interests only. He would love our mindset to be, "What would I like most?" "What can others do for me?" "I will see what kind of pleasure I can obtain from others." In other words, he wants you to be a "taker" instead of a "giver."

> *"Only be careful, and watch yourselves closely so that you do not forget the things your eyes have seen or let them slip from your heart as long as you shall live."*
>
> Deuteronomy 4:9

As a young woman, you need to consider your future and the home you will have one day. Have you been taught things that you will want to pass on to your children? Did the values that your parents instilled in you come from their parents, your grandparents? Will you be passing them along to your children's children one day? Have you stopped to think that what you teach your children could affect many generations of people?   This is your legacy!

How can you raise children who will bring you pleasure?

Proverbs 29:3 *"A man who loves wisdom brings joy to his father."*

Proverbs 22:6 *"Train a child in the way he should go, and when he is old he will not turn from it."*

Proverbs 23:13-14 *"Do not withhold discipline from a child; if you punish him with the rod, he will not die. Punish him with the rod and save his soul from death."*

Proverbs 13:24 *"He who spares the rod hates his son, but he who loves him is careful to discipline him."*

Parents shouldn't make excuses for their children's bad behavior.

Proverbs 20:11 *"Even a child is known by his doings, whether his work be pure and right."* Even very young children know what they are doing and if it is right or wrong!

> *Abraham Lincoln once said,*
>
> *"No one is poor who had a godly mother."*

A functional family of peaceful relationships is of greatest importance, not only to us as individuals but to future generations. Our family role may be our most rewarding role in life.

LESSON 4

FRIENDSHIPS AND RELATIONSHIPS

Relationships with other people can be the source of our greatest joy on earth, our deepest sorrow, or our greatest irritation. But our relationships with other people are of utmost importance in our lives. It's a wonderful thing to share the most intimate parts of our life with a trustworthy friend who has our best interests at heart.

Proverbs cautions us to choose the right kinds of friends, to select our friends and companions with great care.

Proverbs 12:26 *"A righteous man is cautious in friendship..."*

Proverbs 13:20 *"He who walks with the wise grows wise, but a companion of fools suffers harm."*

Proverbs 14:7 *"Stay away from a foolish man, for you will not find knowledge on his lips."*

Proverbs 24:1-2 *"Do not envy wicked men, do not desire their company; for their hearts plot violence, and their lips talk about making trouble."*

We need to choose friends who are good for us, who help us to be better people.

When I was a teenager, my mother used to pray, not only for me but also for my friends, because she knew how much influence they had on my life.

Proverbs 27:17 *"As iron sharpens iron, so one man sharpens another."* Discuss what this means!

That is the kind of friendship we should cultivate!

Proverbs warns us not to stir up dissention or quarrel with each other. The following Scriptures have some interesting word pictures.

Proverbs 30:33 *"For as churning the milk produces butter, and as twisting the nose produces blood, so stirring up anger produces strife."*

Proverbs 17:14 *"Starting a quarrel is like breaching a dam; so drop the matter before a dispute breaks out."*

Proverbs 12:16 *"A fools shows his annoyance at once, but a prudent man overlooks an insult."*

Proverbs 19:11 *"A man's greatest wisdom gives him patience; it is to his glory to overlook an offense."*

Proverbs 17:9 *"He who covers over an offense promotes love..."*

> **True friends are loyal friends. They have integrity. They can be trusted. They are dependable. They are truthful.**

Proverbs 27:10 *"Do not forsake your friend and the friend of your father..."*

Proverbs 25:19 *"Like a bad tooth or a lame foot is reliance on the unfaithful in times of trouble."*

Proverbs 12:22 *"The Lord detests lying lips, but he delights in men who are truthful."*

Proverbs 24:28 *"Do not testify against your neighbor without cause, or use your lips to deceive."*

Proverbs 11:9a *"With his mouth the godless destroys his neighbor."*

> **If a person tells you somebody else's business, that person will tell your business to somebody else.**

Proverbs 11:12-13 *"A man who lacks judgment derides his neighbor, but a man of understanding holds his tongue. A gossip betrays a confidence, but a trustworthy man keeps a secret."*

Proverbs 25:9 *"Do not betray another man's confidence."*

In only 20 years, the spread of HIV/AIDS has grown from 8 million cases to 34 million cases worldwide. The spread of "spiritual sickness", through gossip, can travel just as fast. It can be quite damaging to individuals, friends, families and churches. Each of us should be careful not to spread the sickness of gossip.

To silence gossip, refuse to repeat it. Is this a "natural" tendency?

Proverbs 26:20 *"Without wood a fire goes out; without gossip a quarrel dies down."*

- Wisdom is knowing when to speak your mind and when to mind your speech.
- It takes a wise person to know what not to say—and then not to say it!
- If you hold your tongue at the right time, you won't have to eat your words later.

From **The Daily Bread**, "An elderly gentleman tells this story: 'One day when I was about 8 years of age, I was playing beside an open window while our neighbor confided to my mother a serious problem concerning another person. When our visitor was gone, my mother realized I had heard everything said. 'If Mrs. Brown had left her purse here just now, would you give it to someone else?' 'Why of course not,' I replied. 'Well, she left something more precious than that. The story she told could hurt many people and cause much unhappiness. It still belongs to her, and we shall not pass it on to anyone. Do you understand?' I did, and I have remembered ever since that a confidence or a bit of careless gossip is not mine to distribute to others."

George Washington Carver once said, "How far you go in life depends on your being tender with the young, compassionate with the aged, sympathetic with the striving, and tolerant of the weak and the strong. Because someday in life you will have been all of these."

Proverbs 16:24 *"Kind words are like honey—sweet to the soul and healthy for the body."*

Proverbs 25:11 *"A word aptly spoken is like apples of gold in settings of silver."*

Proverbs 15:23 *"A man finds joy in giving an apt reply—and how good is a timely word."*

Proverbs 12:25 *"An anxious heart weighs a man down, but a kind word cheers him up."*

What a joy it is to see the face of a friend brightened from timely words or advice!

Some people have a special gift of encouragement. Do you know someone in your group who has this trait?

[
A good memory verse:

Proverbs 17:17 "A friend loves at all times,

and a brother is born for adversity."
]

Proverbs 18:24 *"A man of many companions may come to ruin, but there is a friend who sticks closer than a brother."*

Jesus is the best friend we will ever have. Other friends may disappoint us, let us down, fail to care about us, turn their backs on us, or walk off and leave us, but Jesus will always care, always understand, and always be there for us. He is the ultimate model of what a friend should be like, and of what we should be like as friends. He is the *ultimate* friend for each of us!

POWER, PROVIDENCE, PRINCIPLES

Have you ever shown an interest in an activity that you didn't really care about just to connect and spend time with a person who enjoyed that activity? In some cases, we step out of our comfort zone to win the approval of others.

We have a heavenly Father who loves us, and, hopefully, we love him so much that we want his approval and want to do things that bring pleasure to him. Surely, we will likewise want to avoid doing those things that would displease God, things that would make him sad or disappointed in us. This lesson talks about living wisely in the fear of the Lord. When we speak about fearing the Lord, we simply mean reverencing him, living to please him, avoiding what displeases him, putting him first, and coming into alignment with his will.

Three ways we can do that:
1. We accept his **power**, his sovereignty, and his plan for our lives.
2. We acknowledge his **providence** and are grateful for his daily protection and provision.
3. We act on his **precepts and principles**, applying the things we learn in his word.

His Power

It pleases God when we accept his plan and his sovereignty, his power and his control. God is our creator. He has a plan for all of his creation, including you and me, and he has the power to fulfill his plans. He has given us a free will with which we can make many decisions in our lives, but our free will operates under the umbrella of God's sovereignty.

When I took a recent cruise, I was able to move around the ship and choose activities of my liking. All the while I was going about my sunning, games, eating, etc., the ship was on its predetermined course to the next port. So it is with God's sovereignty and man's freedom. They exist together.

God's sovereignty can overrule the freedom of man at any time!

Proverbs 19:21 *"Many are the plans in a man's heart, but it's the Lord's purpose that prevails."*

Proverbs 21:30 *"There is no wisdom, no insight, no plan that can succeed against the Lord."*

Proverbs 27:1 *"Do not boast about tomorrow, for you do not know what a day may bring forth."*

Acknowledging the sovereignty of God includes acknowledging the frailty of man. If we are honest in our comparison of man with God, we will have a spirit of great humility because we are totally dependent upon our creator. Some people may look big and important compared to some other people, but how small we must look when compared to an eternal, all powerful, all wise God, creator of this vast universe and everything in it!

PSALM 104 (selected readings)

"O Lord my God, how great you are! You are robed with honor and with majesty and light! You stretched out the starry curtain of the heavens and hollowed out the surface of the earth to form the seas. The clouds are your chariots. You ride upon the wings of the wind. The angels are your messengers...You bound the world together so that it would never fall apart....You spoke, and at the sound of your shout the water collected into vast ocean beds, and mountains rose and valleys sank to the levels you decreed. And then you set a boundary for the seas, so that they would never again cover the earth. You placed springs in the valleys, and streams that gush from the mountains. They give water for all the animals to drink....You send rain upon the mountains and fill the earth with fruit. The tender grass grows up at your command to feed the cattle, and there are fruit trees, vegetables, and grain for man to cultivate.... You assigned the moon to mark the months, and the sun to mark the days....In your wisdom you have made them all! The earth is full of your riches."

How awesome God is!!!

Prideful people can disbelieve or resent the thought of God's control, but the adventure of the Christian life is in knowing that God desires to involve us, to allow us to partner with him and to be a part of his plan. Some people will only accept the reality that God is in control when it becomes abundantly clear that we are not, when some disaster occurs in our lives.

Proverbs 3:7 *"Do not be wise in your own eyes; fear the Lord and shun evil."*

Proverbs 8:13b *"I hate pride and arrogance, evil behavior and perverse speech."*

Pride is the only disease known to man that makes everyone sick except the person who has it!

When I acknowledge God's place as first in my life, he directs the course of my life to align with his purposes.

Romans 8:28 *"And we know that in all things God works for the good of those who love him, who have been called according to his purpose."*

Christian author, James Dobson, wrote: "Whenever I am tempted to become self-important and authoritative, I'm reminded of what the mother whale said to her baby: when you get to the top and start to blow, that's when you get harpooned!"

HIS PROVIDENCE

It also pleases God when we acknowledge his providence. This is when his loving hand breaks through time and circumstances to give help or direction to his children. He doesn't just sit up in heaven and watch us struggle.

God knew he planned to flood the earth, so he told Noah to build the ark before it started raining. He parted the sea for Moses and the Israelites when they arrived on the shore with the Egyptian army behind them. He put Joseph in an influential position in anticipation of the famine. He closed the lions' mouths for Daniel. These saints trusted that God was working out his plan and providing for them even if their circumstances appeared for awhile to suggest otherwise. Have any of you come through a hard situation and later looked back and realized that God had been with you?

1 Thessalonians 5:18 *"Give thanks in all circumstances, for this is God's will for you in Christ Jesus."*

When the direction of our lives is interrupted, even if it seems unexpected or catastrophic, it may simply be a course adjustment from our heavenly Father, pointing us back toward his plan. We can rest assured that he is still directing our course. In his providence, he will provide whatever we need to go through any situation. He will always be there for us. He will never forsake us.

Soon after the death of my father, my mother was diagnosed with cancer. I sat with her through several of her "all day" chemotherapy treatments. Sometimes I saw things only with my "earthly eyes". I had much anxiety and fear of losing my other parent. My mother's attitude would always bring me

back. She was kind to all who treated her. She never "fretted" or even cried about her situation. She has been a Christian many years and has a close relationship with God. When I asked her how she could be so calm and accepting she said, "I have walked with the Lord a long time and I am not going to quit now; I want to do this well."

His Precepts and Principles

It pleases God when we act on his precepts and principles. Wisdom is knowing which path to take. Integrity is taking it.

Proverbs 15:9 *"The Lord detests the way of the wicked but he loves those who pursue righteousness."*

Proverbs 4:11 *"I guide you in the way of wisdom and lead you along straight paths."*

Proverbs 21:21 *"He who pursues righteousness and love finds life, prosperity and honor."*

Precepts are black and white, do or don't, statements or commands. Principles involve judgment calls. An example of a precept is a sign that says "Speed Limit 35 MPH." But "Drive Carefully" is a principle since it can vary with road or traffic conditions. The more we know about God's Word, the better judgment calls or decisions we can make.

What principles and precepts have we learned so far in Proverbs? What applications do we need to make in our lives? Here is a summary of the main points.

Get *wisdom*.

Trust and *obey* God.

Work *hard*. Be diligent.

Prepare for the *future*.

Be honest. Tell the *truth*. Be a person of integrity.

Be humble and teachable. Profit from *instruction*.

Listen to the instruction of your *parents*.

Be faithful to your *friend*. Don't gossip.

Don't quarrel. Overlook and *forgive* offenses.

Be *kind* to other people.

When we acknowledge God and try to please him, he will give us direction and his wisdom. James 3:17 tells us what our lives will be like. "But the wisdom that comes from heaven is first of all pure; then peace-loving, considerate, submissive, full of mercy and good fruit, impartial and sincere."

LESSON 6

WORK, MONEY AND HONESTY

Do you think God is interested in your "day to day" life? Does he really care if you do well in school and keep your room neat? Is he interested in the way you handle your allowance/money? Is he interested in how you interact with people you see on a daily basis; your teachers, friends and family members?

To say "no" to these questions is to relegate God to a place of little or no importance. To say "yes" to these questions transforms whatever you do into a thing of dignity, high purpose, satisfaction, and excitement.

Ted Engstrom, from The Making of A Christian Leader, "The world needs men who cannot be bought; whose word is their bond; who put character above wealth; who possess opinions and a will; who are larger than their vocations; who do not hesitate to take chances; who will not lose their individuality in a crowd; who will be as honest in small things as in great things; who will make no compromise with wrong; whose ambitions are not confined to their own selfish desires; who will not say they do it 'because everybody else does it'; who are true to their friends through good report and evil report, in adversity as well as in prosperity; who do not believe that shrewdness, cunning and hardheadedness are the best qualities for winning success; who are not ashamed or afraid to stand for the truth when it is unpopular; who say 'no' with emphasis, although the rest of the world says 'yes.'"

There are three characteristics that are greatly desired in work situations according to Proverbs: honesty, hard work, and kindness to others. There are a number of verses that challenge us to be honest in our work relationships.

Proverbs 20:10 *"Differing weights and differing measures- the Lord detests them both."*

Proverbs 20:23 *"The Lord detests differing weights, and dishonest scales do not please him."*

Proverbs 11:1 *"The Lord abhors dishonest scales, but accurate weights are his delight."*

Proverbs 16:8 *"Better a little with righteousness than much gain with injustice."*

If your desire is to be a "fruit bearer", you must be honest! God knows when you have maneuvered, schemed and lied to get to the top.

The father says: "I want an explanation and I want the truth." The daughter replies: "Make up your mind, Dad; you can't have both!"

Proverbs 22:1 *"A good name is more desirable than great riches; to be esteemed is better than silver or gold."*

There are also many verses in Proverbs that emphasize the value of hard work and warn against laziness. (Proverbs refers to the lazy person as a "sluggard." This is a person who refuses to work!)

David Jeremiah wrote, "Billy Graham tells this of his upbringing: 'I was taught that laziness was one of the worst evils, and there was dignity and honor in labor. I could abandon myself enthusiastically to milking the cows, cleaning out the latrines, and shoveling manure, not because they were pleasant jobs, but because sweaty labor held its own satisfaction.' Through godly rearing, Billy Graham developed the valuable character quality of diligence. A diligent man is one who works hard at every task, no matter how important or how menial. He uses his time efficiently and always puts forth his best work…..Against the backdrop of people who avoid work, cut corners, and do half-hearted jobs, a diligent man stands out. Practicing diligence is an excellent way to stand out for Christ at home, in the workplace, and even at church. Today, complete each one of your tasks, however big or small, with diligence."

Proverbs 26:14-15 *"As a door turns on its hinges, so a sluggard turns on his bed. The sluggard buries his hand in the dish; he is too lazy to bring it back to his mouth."*

Proverbs 13:4 *"The sluggard craves and gets nothing, but the desires of the diligent are fully satisfied."*

Proverbs 21:25-26 *"The sluggard's craving will be the death of him, because his hands refuse to work."*

Proverbs 6:6-11 *"Go to the ant, you sluggard; consider its ways and be wise! It has no commander, no overseer or ruler, yet it stores its provisions in summer and gathers its food at harvest. How long will you lie there, you sluggard? When will you get up from your sleep? A little sleep, a little slumber, a little folding of the hands to rest- and poverty will come on you like a bandit and scarcity like an armed man."*

Proverbs 20:13 *"Do not love sleep or you will grow poor; stay awake and you will have food to spare."*

Proverbs 19:15 *"Laziness brings on deep sleep, and the shiftless man goes hungry."*

The best way to hear money jingle in your pocket is to shake a leg!

Proverbs 10:4-5 *"Lazy hands make a man poor, but diligent hands bring wealth. He who gathers crops in summer is a wise son, but he who sleeps during harvest is a disgraceful son."*

Proverbs 20:4 *"A sluggard does not plow in season; so at harvest time he looks but finds nothing."*

The sluggard will not even care for what he has and will make excuses!

Proverbs 12:27 *The lazy do not roast any game, but the diligent feed on the riches of the hunt.*

Proverbs 19:24 *A sluggard buries his hand in the dish; he will not even bring it back to his mouth!*

Proverbs 22:13 *The sluggard says, "There's a lion outside! I'll be killed in the public square!"*

The diligent man is rewarded with the fruit of his labors!

Proverbs 27:18a *The one who guards a fig tree will eat its fruit,*

Proverbs 18:20 *From the fruit of their mouth a person's stomach is filled; with the harvest of their lips they are satisfied.*

Proverbs 21:5 *The plans of the diligent lead to profit as surely as haste leads to poverty.*

Sometimes if we faithfully fulfill small tasks that God gives us, he will later promote us to larger ones. David cared for his flock of sheep as a boy and later rose to be King of Israel. Joshua was Moses' helper and later led the Israelites into the Promised Land. Abraham was obedient to God early on and later God made him the father of his great nation.

"The world is full of willing people: some willing to work and the rest willing to let them."

Proverbs 14:23 *All hard work brings a profit, but mere talk leads only to poverty.*

Proverbs 28:19 *Those who work their land will have abundant food, but those who chase fantasies will have their fill of poverty.*

Proverbs 24:27 *Put your outdoor work in order and get your fields ready; after that, build your house.*

Not only should we be diligent to take care of ourselves and our families but, if we are good workers, we should have enough to share with those less fortunate, and God expects us to be generous with others. Certainly he has been much more than generous with us. He has given us so many good gifts and lavished his love and grace on us!

Proverbs 11:16 *A kindhearted woman gains honor, but ruthless men gain only wealth.*

Proverbs 14:31 *Whoever oppresses the poor shows contempt for their Maker, but whoever is kind to the needy honors God.*

Proverbs 28:27 *Those who give to the poor will lack nothing, but those who close their eyes to them receive many curses.*

Remember, if you commit your work to the Lord you will succeed.

Proverbs 13:7 *"Some rich people are poor, and some poor people have great wealth!"*

Thomas Edison

"I never did anything worth doing by accident, nor did any of my inventions come by accident; they came by work." He also said, "Opportunity is missed by most people because it is dressed in overalls and looks like work."

LESSON 7

INTRODUCTION TO ECCLESIASTES

God included a vast array of people and situations in the Bible. Isn't that encouraging to us as we compare our lives to theirs? We can relate when we see them "rejoicing in the Lord" and we can also relate when we see them struggle. In the book of Ecclesiastes, we see Solomon at his lowest point. This is in contrast to Proverbs where he shared his incredible wisdom.

How many of you have experienced "down times" in your life?

Solomon's purpose in Ecclesiastes was to unlock the mysteries of life. One thousand years before Christ, he was searching for the answers to the big questions people have asked throughout history and are still asking today:

1. Who am I?
2. Where did I come from?
3. Why am I here?
4. Where am I going?
5. Is there meaning to life?
6. Is there a God?
7. Is there life after death?
8. Is life worth living? There are many people who don't think so and who attempt suicide every year. About 10% of those who try actually succeed.

The Declaration of Independence says a person should have the right to "life, liberty, and the pursuit of happiness." Most people pursue happiness in this life. Most want the richest and most fulfilling life they can possibly have. I do. Don't you?

The world offers us much pleasure and temporary satisfaction, but all roads, except

> **Christian author Max Lucado writes, "Mine deep enough in every heart and you'll find it; a longing for meaning, a quest for purpose. As surely as a child breathes, he will someday wonder, 'What is the purpose of my life?'"**

one, are dead end streets as far as answering the ultimate questions in life and giving us eternal joy and purpose. Many people are frustrated and fighting a losing battle because they are trying to find happiness in places where it cannot be found. There is only one right road that leads to lasting joy.

Blaise Pascal, mathematician, physicist, and philosopher said, "There is a God shaped vacuum in the heart of every person that cannot be filled by any created thing but only by the creator himself." Nothing else in our life will satisfy like God.

With what things do we try to satisfy ourselves? How long does the satisfaction last?

King Solomon tried most of the roads that people travel to try to find happiness, meaning and purpose. He came to the conclusion that these things could only be found in a relationship with God. Let's take a look at some of the roads he traveled.

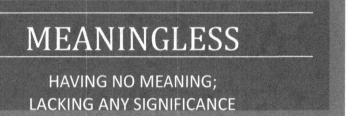

Look at Ecclesiastes chapter one. In verse two, the author said that everything is _meaningless_. Solomon described the futility of life. The phrase "meaningless" expresses the sad belief that life is worthless. He gave us four reasons to support that conclusion. (These are found in Chapters 1 & 2)

Life is boring.

Death is certain.

Wisdom is hopeless.

Wealth is futile.

In Chapter 1:3-10 Solomon talked about the monotony of life. What does this mean to you?

_____

_____

_____

_____

Everything has been tried. We bore easily. This is one reason I enjoy my grand-children so much. It is so much fun to see them experience things for the first time, things that no longer hold the same level of excitement for me.

What phrase does Solomon repeat often? _Under the sun._ This phrase expresses the effort to find everything man needs in **this world**, the human point of view. Things look very different when you see them from God's point of view.

In verse 11 Solomon stated a theme that is echoed throughout this book; death is certain. We are born. We live. We die. Time will roll on, and we will be forgotten. That is life under the sun. **Without God,** this is the sum total of man's hope and future. But **with God**, what wonderful possibilities open up and give us hope for an incredible future with him.

Next Solomon explored the road of wisdom. Remember that God had given him a gigantic portion of wisdom, so if anyone could solve the mysteries of life by human wisdom, it should have been Solomon. But he shows that man's wisdom is limited!

Read Ecclesiastes 1:12-18.

Contrary to human thinking, education will not give man the answers he is seeking to the ultimate questions of life. No amount of human striving can explain life's meaning and purpose.

The next road Solomon went down was pleasure.

Ecclesiastes 2:1-2 *"I thought in my heart, 'Come now, I will test you with pleasure to find out what is good.'"*

> I said to myself, "Let's go for it—experiment with pleasure, have a good time!" But there was nothing to it, nothing but smoke.
>
> What do I think of the fun-filled life? Insane! Insane!
> My verdict on the pursuit of happi-ness? Who needs it?
>
> *Ecclesiastes 2:1-2 (The Message)*

Ecclesiastes 2:10 *"I denied myself nothing my eyes desired; I refused my heart no pleasure."*

But that also proved to be meaningless.

As a teen you might be thinking, "If I just had the right boyfriend, everything would be great." Many times the new wears off. He might make you mad or no longer be as exciting, and you may even break up. People are not perfect; only God is. We should look to God to fill us with peace, joy and satisfaction. God uses people and things to bring us a certain level of happiness, but contentment and abiding joy come from our relationship with God.

Many people go down the road of partying and entertainment. Solomon tried that too.

Ecclesiastes 2:3 *"I tried cheering myself with wine, and embracing folly—my mind still guiding me with wisdom. I wanted to see what was worthwhile for men to do under heaven during the few hours of their lives."*

Solomon also tried the road of building projects, of hard work. Ecclesiastes 2:4-6 *"I undertook great projects; I built houses for myself and planted vineyards. I made gardens and parks and planted all kinds of fruit trees in them. I made reservoirs to water groves of flourishing trees."*

> **It is good to have the things that money can buy, but don't lose the things that money can't buy!**

Solomon tried the road to wealth. Ecclesiastes 2:7-8a, *"I bought male and female slaves and had other slaves who were born in my house. I also owned more herds and flocks than anyone in Jerusalem before me. I amassed silver and gold for myself, and the treasure of kings and provinces."*

Solomon had extreme wealth, beyond anything we could ever imagine. And yet even all that prosperity failed to satisfy him. It has been well said that despair rises out of circumstances of plenty rather than poverty. It is interesting that people who have less of the luxuries and pleasures of life still have the hope that if they had more life would be great. And those who have an abundance of everything the world has to offer realize that it cannot give man inner peace and contentment. Another way to say it might be: the more we have, the more we want, and the more discontented we can become!

Tommy Nelson, in his commentary A Life Well Lived Study Guide: An In-Depth Study of Ecclesiastes, said, "If ever there was a man who could find meaning outside of God, it was Solomon. In terms of intelligence, industry, and accomplishments, he had it all. Solomon used these gifts to accumulate wealth, discover knowledge, and experience pleasure. And he didn't do it in moderation but excess. If Solomon couldn't discover the secret to life, it can't be done."

After Solomon had tried all these things, what was his conclusion about their value?

Ecclesiastes 2:10b-11 *"All was vanity and striving after the wind and there was no profit under the sun."*

Ecclesiastes 2:17   *"So I hated life, for the work which had been done under the sun was grievous to me; because everything is futility and striving after wind."*

Ecclesiastes 2:24-25   *"There is nothing better for a man than to eat and drink and tell himself that his labor is good. This also I have seen, that it is from the hand of God. For who can eat and who can have enjoyment without Him?"*

This lament of Solomon's goes on through chapter 7; then, a turning point occurs in Ecclesiastes 8:12 which says, "Yet surely I know that it shall be well with them that fear God." This is followed up in Ecclesiastes 12:13 which reads, "Fear God, and keep his commandments: for this is the whole duty of man."

> If you look to people and things to satisfy you – you end up distressed,
>
> If you look to circumstances for contentment - you end up depressed,
>
> But when you look to God to fill you – you will be blessed!

When you are feeling down or defeated with your life, open your Bible to Ecclesiastes. There are 12 chapters of pure struggle, written for you, from the wisest man who ever lived. Perhaps you can find parallels in your own hard times and realize that you ARE NOT ALONE. Everyone goes through dark hours, but REJOICE because God is with you! It is in knowing God through Jesus Christ that we find true meaning, purpose and contentment in life and have the hope of an eternal future in heaven.

GOD'S TIME
Ecclesiastes 3:1-14

In the book of Ecclesiastes, Solomon described the emptiness of life apart from God. No matter how random things may seem, in good times or bad, when you can't figure it out, you can take comfort in the truth. God has **a plan for your life**!

GOD IS AT WORK ALL THE TIME

In Ecclesiastes Chapter 3, Solomon clearly stated that God has a plan and does not waver from it. He is the one who has made the appointed time for everything. Solomon began with the familiar verses about the major events and seasons of life by declaring that all human experiences have a place in God's plan – birth, death, laughter, tears, war and peace.

Read Ecclesiastes 3:1-8

Ecclesiastes 3:1 "There is a time for everything, and everything of earth has its _special season_."

Times and seasons are a regular part of life. From before our birth to the moment of our death, God is accomplishing his divine purpose. Ecclesiastes 8:6a "For there is a proper time and procedure for every matter."

Ecclesiastes 3:2a "There is a time to be _born_ and a time to _die_."

Have you ever thought it might be fun to live in another time period? Our birth and death are not happenstance. They are divine appointments. We live in this generation by his perfect timing. We were born into our specific family by God's plan.

Evangelist Billy Graham said, "Life is brief, and it can end in an instant. That's why we must never take life for granted but see every minute as a gift from God to be used for His glory."

Psalm 139:16 *"All the days ordained for me are written in your book."*

Ecclesiastes 3:2b "There is a time to *plant* and *a* time to *harvest."*

Planting and harvesting make an interesting parallel to birth and death. A successful farmer must do both according to the seasons. He knows nature works for him only if he works with nature. Who can give an example of a gardening "rule of thumb?" *Sow seeds and plant bulbs in the proper season. Plants need sunlight and water, etc.*

The secret to a successful life is to learn God's principles and cooperate with them.

Ecclesiastes 3:3 "There is a time to *kill* and a time to *heal."*

Life seems to take place somewhere between a battlefield and a first aid station! When do you think it is an appropriate time to kill?

Ecclesiastes 3:4 "There is a time to *cry* and a time to *laugh*. There is a time to be *sad* and a time to *dance."*

These emotions should always be used at the appropriate time. They are used to show others your reaction to a situation. How much fun is it to share a laugh with friends when they are happy? How consoling is it to have a friend share your sadness or tears?

"TURN! TURN! TURN!"

"Turn! Turn! Turn! (to Everything There Is a Season)" is a song adapted entirely from the *Book of Ecclesiastes* in the Bible (with the exception of the last line) and put to music by Pete Seeger in 1959.

The song became an international hit in late 1965 when it was covered by the American folk rock band The Byrds, reaching #1 on the *Billboard* Hot 100 chart. The Byrds' version of the song easily holds the record for the #1 hit with the oldest lyrics.

Proverbs 10:11 *"The words of a good person give life, like a fountain of water, but the words of the wicked contain nothing but violence."*

Proverbs 15:4 *"As a tree gives fruit, healing words give life, but dishonest words crush the spirit."*

Proverbs 26:20 *"Being happy-go-lucky around a person whose heart is heavy is as bad as stealing his jacket in cold weather, or rubbing salt in his wounds."*

Ecclesiastes 3:5a "There is a time to *throw away* stones and a time to *gather* them." A farmer will need to dispose of small stones when cultivating his field. He might gather the larger ones and keep them to build fences or buildings. This example of "sorting" can be used in many areas of life. Can you think of an example?

Ecclesiastes 3:5b "There is a time to hug and a time not to hug."

Ecclesiastes 3:6a "There is a time to *look for something* and a time to *stop looking for something*." Some translations say "to give up as lost."
Why would you decide this?

Ecclesiastes 3:6b "There is a time to *keep things* and a time to *throw things away*." Have you ever seen the show "Hoarders?" We need to be wise in finding the right time to get rid of things.

Ecclesiastes 3:7a "There is a time to *tear* apart and a time to *sew* together." The Jews tore their clothing in times of grief. Joel 2:13 "Rend your heart and not your garments and turn unto the Lord." God expects us to have sorrow during bereavement but not like unbelievers, who have no hope. There also comes a time to "get over it" and sew it up!

Ecclesiastes 3:7b "There is a time to *be silent* and a time to *speak*." If God has told you to be silent you need to heed his advice. There are also times you need to speak up!

Ecclesiastes 3:8 "There is a time to *love* and a time to *hate*." There are some times that even Christians are to hate. Psalm 97:10 "Let those who love the Lord hate evil." Read Proverbs 6:16-19. Find seven things that God hates. (Hatred should be aimed at the sin, not the sinner.)

1.

2.

3.

4.

5.

6.

7.

"There is a time for _war_ and a time for _peace_."   When would a time for war be appropriate?

Read Ecclesiastes 3:9-14. What does Solomon share in these verses that he concludes about life?

We may not understand God's ways, but we can trust him. He will make everything beautiful in its time. In this life we should find satisfaction in his gifts and in worshiping him. We should do all the good we can and trust the future to him.

We see the ugly cocoon – God sees the beautiful butterfly. We see today – he's working on forever. He makes everything beautiful in its time – your loss, your heartaches, your trials, your battles, your illnesses, and your failures.

Romans 8:28 _"And we know that in all things God works for the good of those who love him, who have been called according to his purpose."_

How can hard times or sad times work for our good?

We should not portray the Christian life as "smooth sailing" all the time. The Bible tells us that our lives will be seasons of ups and downs.

God is wise!   Even bad things can be used to help us become the Christians he created us to be!

LESSON 9

THE BEATITUDES
Matthew 5:1-12

All people pursue happiness. Some look to the entertainment industry--movies, theater, television and sports. Others may search for happiness in food and drink. Some spend money and some travel to acquire happiness. Still others look to their boyfriends or partners for their joy. That kind of happiness brings temporary satisfaction. Jesus pointed to a source of lasting happiness. In the Sermon on the Mount, he listed some spiritual qualities that characterize the truly happy person. Believers find these qualities in a life of submission, trust, obedience, and faithfulness to God. Happiness depends on what we **are**, not on what we have or what we do or where we go!

Jesus told us the inward qualities that should be found in the life of a Christian in his much loved sermon. The word "beatitude" means "blessing" and comes from the Latin word for blessed. Blessed means "how happy," "how fortunate," and "to be congratulated." The beatitudes are the attitudes that ought to be in our lives if we are true Christians.

be·at·i·tude

noun \bē-ˈa-tə-ˌtüd, -ˌtyüd\

Etymology: derived from Latin *beatus* "happy, blessed"

Definition: 1: a state of utmost bliss

2: any of the declarations made in the Sermon on the Mount (Matthew 5:3-11) beginning "Blessed are"

Do you think there are people today who "pretend" to be holy? People whose walk doesn't match their talk?

Who were the Pharisees?

The Pharisees emphasized outward behavior, but Jesus emphasized the inner attitudes and motives of the heart. The Pharisees and teachers of the law kept the **letter of the law**, but Jesus is showing by his life and his teachings that keeping the **spirit of the law** is much more important.

Read Matthew 5:1-3

The "poor in spirit" are those who are humble, who realize how weak and sinful they are. They know that they are spiritually bankrupt apart from Christ and realize how spiritually wealthy they are with him. Their attitude is just the opposite of the proud, self-sufficient, self-righteous attitude of the Scribes and Pharisees. As a reward, the poor in spirit receive the kingdom of heaven. Because they recognize and acknowledge their need for God's power and sovereignty in their lives, they receive it. God accepts and directs people who express their need of him and commit their lives to him.

SELF EXAMINE—Is this an area in your life that could use some work? Do you humbly and submissively come to God for help or do you try to make it under your own power?

_____

_____

_____

Read Matthew 5:4

The mourning in this verse is a sincere sorrow for sin, the kind of sorrow that leads to repentance. God forgives and comforts us when we approach him in true repentance. Peter mourned with a true godly sorrow and was forgiven. Judas had only a worldly kind of sorrow, regret without repentance, and took his own life.

SELF EXAMINE—When you ask God for forgiveness, are you just trying to "get out of trouble" or make yourself "feel better" or are you deeply disturbed that you have disconnected your fellowship with God by sinning?

_____

_____

_____

Read Matthew 5:5

Meekness is not weakness. The word translated "meek" was used by the Greeks to describe a horse that had been broken. It refers to power under control. Meekness means not asserting our own rights but living for the glory of God. It is the opposite of self will.

SELF EXAMINE—Think of a time that you gave up your own right (or desire) to live for the glory of God. Share if you like.

_____

_____

_____

Read Matthew 5:6

A true Christian has an appetite for spiritual things. There's no reason to let our hunger for spiritual nourishment go unsatisfied! Christ, the Bread of Life, satisfies our spiritual hunger when we come to him and feast on his word!

SELF EXAMINE—Do you have a deep longing to spend time with God through regular prayer and Bible reading? (Don't forget you are involved in this study!) _This would be a good time to share about your daily quiet time and let anyone else share about theirs._

_____

_____

_____

Read Matthew 5:7

This is the law of the harvest--we reap what we sow. God has been faithful to show us mercy in saving us when we were sinners. He expects us to pass the mercy of forgiveness along to others.

SELF EXAMINE—Is there someone you need to forgive? Remember what you ask in the Lord's Prayer: forgive me my trespasses as I forgive those that trespass against me!

_____

_____

_____

Read Matthew 5:8

The person who is pure in heart has a single heart. His heart is not divided between God and the world. His heart has unmixed motives and focuses on devotion to God. The person who is focused on God above all else will be able to see his heavenly Father in a unique way.

SELF EXAMINE—If you were to honestly examine your devotion to God, what percentage of your heart would you say he possesses?

_____

_____

_____

Read Matthew 5:9

Peace makers are not simply peace lovers. They are involved in resolving conflicts. They are part of the solution, not the problem. Sometimes this takes risk, and, as a peacemaker, you might be injured in the crossfire. Peacemakers take the risk and stay with the job because they want to serve and honor God.

Read Matthew 5:10-12

How do you react to opposition in your Christian life? You can become a martyr and feel sorry for yourself. You can become angry and fight back. You can react in fear and back away from any public stand for Christ. But true righteousness stands firm in the face of opposition and discovers that God's powerful presence strengthens and sustains us if we exhibit the courage to speak up on his behalf.

SELF EXAMINE—Am I able to stand boldly for Christ during opposition to him? Do I have the scriptural knowledge needed to make an adequate response/defense?

_____

_____

_____

The Holy Spirit enables us to experience the true righteousness expressed in the Beatitudes in our daily lives. This does not mean that we live sinless, perfect lives. What it does mean is that, if we yield ourselves completely to him, Christ will live his life through us by the power of his Spirit. The only way we can experience this true righteousness is through the power of Jesus Christ. The Beatitudes give us a clear picture of what a true disciple of Christ should be like.

JESUS TAUGHT US TO PRAY
Matthew 6

In the last chapter, we studied about the true righteousness that characterizes a child of God. We saw that the righteousness of the Pharisees was insincere, hypocritical and self centered. They practiced their religion for the applause of men, not for the desire to please God. In this lesson we will see true righteousness applied in the everyday activities of life. In Matthew chapter 6 we see several different areas of life that test whether a person is sincerely desiring to please God or seeking the approval and praise of other people.

In Matthew 6:1-18 Jesus addressed three areas in the Christian life: giving, praying and fasting. He followed the same four point outline for all three areas.
1. A warning not to do these things for the praise of men.
2. An assurance that those who seek the praise of men will get only the earthly reward of man's approval.
3. A command to give, pray and fast in private.
4. A promise that God, who sees in secret, will reward us openly.

Read Matthew 6:1-4 and notice the four points of the outline.

1._____

2._____

3._____

4._____

IT IS POSSIBLE TO DO THE RIGHT THING WITH THE WRONG MOTIVE!

Giving to the poor, praying and fasting were important disciplines in the Jewish religion. Jesus certainly approved of these practices. In fact, he assumed that people would give, pray and fast, but he cautioned people to be sure their hearts were right as they practiced these different parts of religion.

Can you name any local organizations that publish donor lists? Are donors categorized according to the size of their contributions? These lists can appeal to man's desire for recognition. Jesus said giving to be noticed was like announcing one's gifts "with trumpets." Some might call this "tooting your own horn."

> The following is taken from *The Daily Bread*, December 28, 1998, entitled <u>Secret Service</u> written by David C. Egner. "When we serve God in secret, we receive a double reward. Not only will God one day reward us 'openly', but we will enjoy the memory of what we did." Thomas LaMance wrote: "Several years back...I was lounging around in the living room listening to the radio when my dad came in from shoveling snow. He looked at me and said, 'In 24 hours you won't even remember what you were listening to now. How about doing something for the next 20 minutes that you'll remember the next twenty years? I promise that you'll enjoy it every time you think of it.' 'What is it?' I asked. 'Well, son, there are several inches of snow on Mrs. Brown's walk,' he replied. 'Why don't you go see if you can shovel it off and get back home without her knowing you did it?' I did the walk in about 15 minutes. She never knew who did the job, and my dad was right. It's been a lot more than 20 years, and I've enjoyed the memory every time I've thought about it."

How could you avoid this when it comes to giving?
Give anonymously. Help in ways that do not draw attention to yourself.

Jesus talked about giving to be seen by men. Next He talks about praying to be seen and heard by men.

Read Matthew 6:5-6 *"And when you pray, do not be like the hypocrites, for they love to pray standing in the synagogues and on the street corners to be seen by others. Truly I tell you, they have received their reward in full. But when you pray, go into your room, close the door and pray to your Father, who is unseen. Then your Father, who sees what is done in secret, will reward you."*

Jesus gave us four guidelines for effective prayer in this passage:

Guideline 1: Part of our prayer must be in secret. Public prayer is just the tip of the iceberg. Our private prayer life should be much deeper and more intimate than our public prayer life.

Guideline 2: We must pray sincerely, without hypocrisy, not to be heard by men but to speak to God.

We read about a particular kind of insincere prayer in Matthew 6:7. What does it tell us? *"And when you pray, do not keep on babbling like pagans, for they think they will be heard because of their many words."*

It is possible to treat what we call The Lord's Prayer this way—just recite the familiar words without thinking about them. Jesus didn't give us this prayer to be memorized and then recited over and over. He gave us this prayer to help us think about what we are praying, to keep us from using vain repetitions. He didn't tell us to pray in these specific words. He said, "This, then, is how you should pray." This prayer is designed as a pattern for our prayers. It could be called the "Model Prayer" since we should pray according to it.

Matthew 6:8 *"Do not be like them, for your Father knows what you need before you ask him. "*

Why do we ask God for things if He already knows what we need?

James 4:2b *"You do not have because you do not ask God."*

In the Lord's Prayer, our Model Prayer, notice that there are no singular pronouns. They are all plural. It begins with <u>our</u> Father. We are part of God's worldwide family of believers. You shouldn't be thinking "Lord bless Dad, Mom, brother and me, us four and no more." It is really a privilege and a joy to be an intercessor for other members of the family of believers. How exciting it is when you see God answer a prayer you have prayed on someone's behalf. Prayer is a "family affair." We are just children addressing our Father. How wonderful that we as believers can choose at any time to enjoy a conversation and fellowship with the King of Kings!

Guideline 3: We must pray for God's will. Matthew 6:9b-10 *"Our Father in heaven, hallowed be your name, your kingdom come, your will be done on earth as it is in heaven."*

It is proper to put God's concerns first and then bring him our needs. The Lord's Prayer does not begin, "Our Father, give me." Prayer should be more than a wish list or a "to do" list we present to God.

In Alexander Solzhenitsyn's book, <u>A Day in the Life of Ivan Denisovich</u>, "Ivan endures all the horrors of a Soviet prison camp. One day he is praying with his eyes closed when a fellow prisoner notices him and says with ridicule, 'Prayers won't help you get out of here any faster.' Opening his eyes, Ivan answers, 'I do not pray to get out of prison but to do the will of God.'"

It pleases God for us to ask him to meet our needs. He has designed prayer to be the way through which these needs are met. So we pray the equivalent of "Give us our daily bread." We should do more than pray generic, all encompassing prayers, like "Please bless everybody in the whole world." God likes us to be very specific about our needs so we can clearly see when he has given us a very specific answer.

"Bread" represents the necessities of life, not the luxuries. We probably need a lot less than we want. God gives us a promise in Philippians 4:19: "And my God will meet all your needs according to his glorious riches in Christ Jesus."

Guideline 4: We must pray with a forgiving spirit toward others. So we should pray the equivalent of verse 12 which says: *"Forgive us our debts, as we also have forgiven our debtors."*

Matthew 6:14-15 is very plain about forgiveness also. It says: *"For if you forgive men when they sin against you, your heavenly Father will also forgive you. But if you do not forgive men their sins, your Father will not forgive your sins."*

So if we want to be forgiven, we must forgive others! We will never have to forgive others as much as God has forgiven us.

Now look back at verse 13. It may seem like a strange request, "and lead us not into temptation, but deliver us from the evil one," or "from evil." We know that God will never tempt us to do evil. We realize our own weakness against the enemy, and we wisely pray that God will deliver us from yielding to Satan's advances.

The Lord's Prayer begins and ends with praise. It acknowledges the greatness of God. Some versions begin and end with, "Hallowed be thy name" and "for thine is the kingdom and the power and the glory, forever." Praise and thanksgiving are very important parts of our prayers. Do you praise and thank God often?

LESSON 11

THE LOVE CHAPTER

"And now these three remain: faith, hope and love. But the greatest of these is love" 1 Corinthians 13:13

You might like to research and give the students a brief history of the town of Corinth during the time of Paul's writing. This letter tends to deal with problems of behavior within the Christian church. Read the entire chapter aloud and ask the students to select their favorite verse or verses as you read. At the end of the reading, go around the group and let each student share which verse was her favorite.

1 Corinthians 13:1-13

This familiar passage is often used at weddings. It can be lifted out of Scripture and stand beautifully on its own. This chapter could be described as Paul's finest work. Every time I read these beautiful words my heart is moved. This amazing passage motivates me to put aside my fleshly desires. I long to love in the way my heavenly Father does. I always seem to fall so short of the mark, even though I desire his perfection.

Paul was actually using this writing to try to unify the church in Corinth. In some of the earlier chapters, Paul was stressing unity by urging them to love. Flip back through the first twelve chapters of the book of Corinthians and cite examples of this. *Students will find many.*

In 1 Corinthians 12, the previous chapter, Paul was writing about spiritual gifts and trying to correct some of the abuses of these gifts. (See 1 Corinthians 12:31) *"But eagerly desire the greater gifts."*

Read 1 Corinthians 13:1   *"If I could speak in the tongues of men and of angels, but have not love, I am only a resounding gong or a clanging cymbal."*

Paul was saying that if he could speak in every language of men and even the heavenly language of angels but didn't have love, he would only be *making noise.* He compared the noise to that of a gong or a clashing cymbal, which were commonly used in pagan ritual dances for heathen gods. They made plenty of noise but no melody. *Discuss. Could some people be considered that way?*

Read 1 Corinthians 13:2   *"If I have the gift of prophecy and can fathom all mysteries and all knowledge, and if I have a faith that can move mountains, but have not love, I am nothing."*

Who might this remind you of in our earlier studies? *King Solomon*

Paul turned from knowledge and deeds of power in verse 2 to deeds of mercy and dedication in verse 3.

Read 1 Corinthians 13:3 *"If I give all I possess to the poor and surrender my body to the flames, but have not love, I gain nothing."*

These are extreme acts of selflessness but would still profit a person nothing without love.

What are three characteristics of love that show why it is so important in ministry?

Love is *enriching.* Verses 1-3 show us that a ministry without love is worth absolutely nothing, but with love the ministry enriches the whole church. In fact, love enriches all it touches.

Love is *edifying.* Look at 1 Corinthians 8:1b *"Knowledge puffs up, but love builds up."* Verses in 1 Corinthians 13:4-7 show us how love builds others up! It is love applied. *Read these.*

Love is *enduring.* What love produces, lasts. It will be gold, silver and precious stones rather than wood, hay and stubble.   When gifts are exercised with love, they become productive, effective and fruitful.

Read 1 Corinthians 13:8 *"Love never fails. But where there are prophecies, they will cease; where there are tongues, they will be stilled; where there is knowledge, it will pass away."*

There are different opinions today in the body of Christ as to when the sign gifts such as tongues, prophecy in the sense of foretelling, healing, and miracles pass away. Some believe that God used these gifts in the early church and before scripture was written, and they are no longer needed or valid today. Others believe that these gifts are to be used today and until Christ comes again, which will then make them obsolete.

Paul gave some analogies concerning what will happen when Christ returns, or when we die and go to heaven, if that happens before his return.

Read 1 Corinthians 13:9-11 *"For we know in part and we prophesy in part, but when perfection comes, the imperfect disappears. When I was a child, I talked like a child, I thought like a child, I reasoned like a child. When I became a man, I put childish ways behind me. Now we see but a poor reflection as in a mirror; then we shall see face to face. Now I know in part; then I shall know fully, even as I am fully known."*

Our knowledge will one day be complete. Paul exercised his maturity with determination. Childish things don't just pass away. *Have students think of examples of adults using childish means to get their way. Spending too much time in front of the TV or playing instead of taking care of your family.* The verb which Paul used indicates his determination not to be ruled by childish attitudes. It is in the perfect tense, which indicates that Paul put these things away with decision and finality.

The next analogy used was seeing through a poor mirror. What do you think mirrors were like in Paul's time? They were probably made of polished metal and the images weren't very clear. In this life, our view is dim and distorted, but one day we will see with perfect clarity.

Have you thought of a list of questions that you would like to ask God when you get to heaven?

Read 1 Corinthians 13:13 *"And now these three remain: faith, hope and love. But the greatest of these is love."*

Faith, hope and love are the supreme virtues, but the greatest is love, partially because of its endurance. When we get to heaven, faith will be replaced by *sight,* and hope will be replaced by *possession,* but love will control *all that God's redeemed people do and say*.

Let's go back and read this passage and insert Jesus where you see the word love and see how perfectly it fits. Now insert your name in verses 4 through 7. Sound funny? We have a long way to go but a wonderful goal.

If I speak in the tongues of men or of angels, but do not have _____, I am only a resounding gong or a clanging cymbal.

If I have the gift of prophecy and can fathom all mysteries and all knowledge, and if I have a faith that can move mountains, but do not have _____, I am nothing.

If I give all I possess to the poor and give over my body to hardship that I may boast, but do not have _____, I gain nothing.

_____ is patient, _____ is kind. It does not envy, it does not boast, it is not proud.

It does not dishonor others, it is not self-seeking, it is not easily angered, it keeps no record of wrongs.

_____ does not delight in evil but rejoices with the truth.

It always protects, always trusts, always hopes, always perseveres.

_____ never fails. But where there are prophecies, they will cease; where there are tongues, they will be stilled; where there is knowledge, it will pass away.

For we know in part and we prophesy in part,

but when completeness comes, what is in part disappears.

When I was a child, I talked like a child, I thought like a child, I reasoned like a child. When I became a man, I put the ways of childhood behind me.

For now we see only a reflection as in a mirror; then we shall see face to face. Now I know in part; then I shall know fully, even as I am fully known.

And now these three remain: faith, hope and _____. But the greatest of these is _____.

LESSON 12

SPIRITUAL GIFTS

Have these props ready for a skit: a pillow, a magazine, a book, some flowers and an envelope with a $ drawn on the front. The purpose of this lesson is to help students discover their spiritual gift/gifts. Our scripture is found in 1 Corinthians 12. Say to students: This may be one of the most interesting and helpful lessons we have ever had. We are talking about spiritual gifts. Every believer has at least one, and many have more than one. These were given to us when we trusted Christ and they are to be used for the good of the body of believers.

Read 1 Corinthians 12:1-11.

Each believer has at least one spiritual gift and many have more than one! Every person must function in other areas as well as those in which they are gifted. All Christians are expected to give, to witness, to offer hospitality to others, to show mercy to those in need, etc. God won't let us get away with saying we aren't going to do something because it is not our gift. People will tend to enjoy functioning in the areas of their gifts more than in other areas and will be more efficient and effective in those areas. So our primary ministry should be in the area where we are especially gifted to serve!

Have you ever noticed that you are just more "comfortable" in certain roles of work and service? Have you ever been frustrated or even jealous that you are not "better" in different areas? *Discuss*

The Bible gives us two warnings about gifts:

    1 Corinthians 12:1 *We should not be ignorant about our gifts.*
    1 Timothy 4:14 *Do not neglect your gift.*

Sometimes you have to try out different forms of service to discover your gift, or gifts. Once discovered, you should develop your gift, which is hard work.

There are different opinions on what are and are not spiritual gifts. Some people consider such things as music, art and prayer as spiritual gifts.

If we all made a list of our interpretation of what the Bible offers as "gifts", our lists would probably be a little different.

This is a suggested list, and it is divided it into three categories.

SPIRITUAL GIFTS

Support Gifts	Service Gifts	Sign Gifts
Apostleship	Administration	Miracles
Prophecy	Exhortation	Healing
Evangelism	Faith	Tongues
Pastor—Teacher	Giving	Interpretation of Tongues
Teaching	Helping	
Discerning Spirits	Showing Mercy	
	Hospitality	

The Support Gifts are the gifts that support the body of believers like bones support the human body. They have several characteristics in common:

- People with Support Gifts usually exercise these gifts to a group of people.
- Support Gifts have to do with communicating Scripture.
- These gifts help equip the saints for service.

The Service Gifts are the gifts that build up and encourage and strengthen the body of believers just like muscles in the human body.

- They are generally exercised away from the limelight or behind the scenes.
- They focus on other people.

The Sign Gifts are given to honor and praise God. Different denominations and individuals feel differently about "if and how" these gifts are used today.

1 Corinthians 12:7 emphasizes that the spiritual gifts are given for _the common good_ of the body. The human body is better off when all areas are exercised. Since God has given each of us gifts, he has a ministry for us in the exercising of these gifts.

Let's look at the gifts and see if we can zero in on the characteristics and pick your gift out! You may also be able to pick out gifts of people you know well and perhaps understand them better.

Your gifts should be things you most enjoy doing. You should be the most efficient and the most effective in these areas. Your function in your gifts seems to flow easily and produce satisfaction. While hard work may be involved, the exercising of your gifts is not so much a chore as a joy and a pleasure. You probably have been asked by others to function in the area of your spiritual gifts because they recognize your ability there!

Let's look at the different gifts from the chart.

APOSTLESHIP

Generally speaking, an apostle is one who is sent forth, and in that sense we would qualify, but technically speaking these were the original twelve apostles of Christ.

- They had witnessed the resurrected Christ.
- Their ministries were authenticated by miracles and signs.
- Their word was authoritative.
- They were the founders of the early church and writers of much of the New Testament.

PROPHECY

In the years before the establishment of the New Testament church, the prophets brought a word directly from God. They would tell of a new revelation or foretell of a future event. Prophecy means not only "foretell" but also "forth tell" --tell forth the gospel message. It is the proclamation of the word of God in the wisdom and power of the Holy Spirit. In this sense, it continues as a gift in the church today.

TEACHING

This is the ability to communicate scriptural truth with accuracy, clarity, wisdom and simplicity. A gifted teacher makes what the Bible says clear. A teacher is a guardian of the truth. He doesn't usually originate anything new but defines, describes and declares existing revelation.

How many of you possibly see yourselves in a teaching role in the future?

PASTOR–TEACHER

While the teacher guards the truth, the pastor guards the flock. He nourishes and protects the people in it, encouraging them and ministering to them with sensitivity to their particular needs.

FAITH

This isn't the kind of faith that brings us to salvation. All Christians have that. This is the ability to trust God without doubt or disturbance regardless of circumstances. People of faith aren't surprised when God answers prayers. These people are good cheer leaders and encouragers to others.

GIVING

We are certainly all expected to give, but the person with the gift of giving is sensitive to the needs of others and provides for them with great joy and generosity. People with the gift of giving often live modestly, spending minimum amounts on themselves because they prefer to give to others. Sometimes the ability to make money may accompany the gift of giving, but people do not have to be wealthy to exercise this gift. Remember the "giving widow" in the Bible. What did she give to the temple? *All she had.*

HELPING OR SERVING

This is the ability to assist and support others in the family of God in practical ways with great faithfulness and delight. These people tend to stay in the background but are essential to leaders.

EXHORTATION

This word can mean to encourage, urge, advise and even to caution. This is what mothers do to get their kids to shape up! Exhorters are anxious to see other people live up to their potential. These people make good counselors.

EVANGELISM

These people have a burning desire to see people come to Christ. Everywhere they go they are sharing the gospel and seeing people become Christians. Can you think of any examples?

DISCERNMENT

This is the ability to distinguish right from wrong, good from evil, true from false, real from counterfeit.

HOSPITALITY

This person opens her home to others and sees to it that they feel at ease and welcome.

SHOWING MERCY

This is a compassionate person. Such people have the ability to empathize with the needs, pains, heartaches, disappointments and sorrows of others and to be an agent of healing and comfort. These people are good at visiting the sick, at helping the down and out, and organizing programs to meet the needs of others. Can you think of any examples?

ADMINISTRATION

This person is visionary, goal-oriented, decisive, calm, clear thinking and practical. The administrator has the ability to preside, govern, plan and organize with wisdom, fairness, kindness and efficiency. These people specialize in details and logistics.

SPIRITUAL GIFTS SKIT

This skit will show us some examples of these spiritual gifts in action. Seven women have gone to visit their friend, Cindy Sickly. Each of the women has a different spiritual gift and responds to the illness of the friend in a way characteristic of her gift. *Assign the 8 parts. Mary gets the pillow, Hannah the magazine, Helen the flowers, Terri gets the book and Gracie the $ envelope. Cindy Sickly can be lying down.*

MARY MERCY: (brings a pillow), I'm so sorry you haven't been feeling well. Here, let me put this pillow behind your back. Can I close the curtain so the sun doesn't get in your eyes?

HANNAH HELPER: (hands Cindy Sickly a magazine), I brought you a magazine. While I'm here, I can call and get your assignments and feed the dog. How about I cook you some dinner also?

CINDY SICKLY: Thanks for the help Hannah, but do you know how to cook?

HELEN HOSPITALITY: (Brings the flowers) I brought you some flowers from my garden to put by your bed. Would you like me to watch the door to see if any other visitors arrive? I can entertain them if you don't feel up to company.

GRACIE GIVING: I heard that your dad's out of work. I have taken up a collection. I hope this will help cover the costs. (She hands an envelope with money to Cindy.)

TERRI TEACHER: (Thumbing through her book)   I have been looking up your symptoms in my medical book.   I think I see the problem and can explain the different treatments.

FRANCES FAITH: I just know Cindy will be well in no time at all! I have been praying for her. She will be up and around in just a day or two; I am sure of it.

ANNIE ADMINISTRATOR: I have talked to your teachers and have all your assignments ready to pick up. I have notified the senior class committee that you will not be at the meeting tomorrow but arranged to have a report emailed to you. Do you have anything else pressing?

CINDY SICKLY: Meeting tomorrow? What meeting?

HELEN HOSPITALITY: We were to meet at the gym but I have changed the meeting to my house tomorrow to discuss prom decorations. I've already ordered pizza and baked brownies. I even invited the new girl to join us since she doesn't know many people.

MARY MERCY: Oh, I'm so glad. I remember just how lonesome I was when I first came to town. I can't wait to meet her and help her get to know everyone so she won't feel so lonely.

ANNIE ADMINISTRATOR: I'll make sure everyone knows it's at Helen's house now. I've already talked to our class president, and she has an agenda ready.

GRACIE GIVING: I have made a small donation toward the prom and will be collecting more money. I want us to get a good band and have really great decorations this year.

FRANCES FAITH: I just know it will be over the top!

HANNA HELPER: I can bring some folding chairs to the meeting. I think we will have a crowd.

TERRI TEACHER: I have looked over the agenda myself and it looks like everything is included to make the meeting a success. Cindy, you just read your magazine and rest. Don't worry about anything.

ALL: Hope you feel better soon. Bye.

Do you see how the different roles compliment the group as a whole? Do you know now what your gift is? Can you pick out the gifts for others in our group? Discuss.

(Your students might enjoy and benefit from taking a spiritual gifts TEST for your NEXT LESSON. There are many good ones found on the internet.)

DAVID'S CONFESSION
Psalm 32 and 51

Psalm 32:1 "Blessed is he whose transgressions are forgiven, whose sins are covered."

Study and share with the students the story of David, Bathsheba and Uriah from 2 Samuel 11.

2 Samuel 11:27b, "But the thing David had done displeased the Lord."

David has been called "a man after God's own heart." He wrote most of the Psalms and walked closely with God, yet the Bible reveals to us the story of his sinful act with Bathsheba and against Uriah, her husband. Why do you think God inspired man to include this account? (As an example to us that even the Godliest of men will be tempted by sin and sometimes fall short of God's standards. He is also used as a beautiful picture of a heart's desire to have a restored fellowship with God.)

Our lesson today has great significance for each of us. What should we do when we sin? How can we avoid sin? How can we be forgiven and restored to fellowship with God? *Confess our sin. Repent. And, ask God's forgiveness. Walk daily with God. God will forgive if we ask and restore our fellowship with Him.*

How would you define sin? *It is disobeying God, which results in a broken relationship with him. Not doing as the Bible, God's holy word, instructs you to do.*

How do you feel when you know you have sinned? *Encourage students to go deep with their descriptions.*

Nathan, the prophet, was sent by God to confront David. Read 2 Samuel 12:1-13. *How would you like Nathan's job? Do you think God might use you at some time to help another person see his sin and get rid of it?*

David wrote Psalm 32 and 51 in connection with his adultery with Bathsheba and the murder of her husband Uriah. These psalms give us insight into David's response to being confronted with his sins. After the confrontation, David turned to God in sincere repentance. He told Nathan, "I have sinned against the Lord." How might some people respond when confronted with their sin? *Some will blame others or use the excuse "everybody does it."*

David poured out in detail his confession of guilt and request for forgiveness in Psalm 51:1-3.

> "Have mercy on me, O God, according to your unfailing love; according to your great compassion blot out my transgressions. Wash away all my iniquity and cleanse me from my sin. For I know my transgressions, and my sin is always before me."
>
> —King David

In this passage, David used three words for sin:

- *Iniquity*, something perverse and crooked.

- *Transgression*, deliberate rebellion against God's will.

- *Sin*, failing to measure up to God's standard of perfection.

David did not blame others for his sin. He took responsibility when he said, "my iniquity", "my sin" and "my transgressions." David asked God to wash away, cleanse, and blot out his sins, to clean him thoroughly and remove his sins from the record.

Read Psalm 51:1-2.   What **three** aspects of God's forgiveness do you find in these verses?

> *Blot out. This means to forgive, to lift our sins off our shoulders and to roll them away.*
> *Wash away. This means he covers the sins with Jesus' blood, protecting the sinner from punishment.*
> *Cleanses us. He cancels our sin debt on heaven's ledger.*

Read Psalm 51:4 *"Against you, you only, have I sinned and done what is evil in your sight, so that you are proved right when you speak and justified when you judge."*

Other people are hurt by our sins, but it is God's law we break when we sin, and all sin is ultimately against him.

Read Psalm 51:5 *"Surely I was sinful at birth, sinful from the time my mother conceived me."*

Who's been around a baby lately? How do babies act?   They cry when they want something!   Everything is on their time table. Do you know people who continue to act that way past the infant stage?

Read Psalm 51:7 *"Cleanse me with hyssop, and I will be clean; wash me, and I will be whiter than snow."*

David's confession continued.   Hyssop was the little shrub the Jews used to put blood on the doorposts at the first Passover in Egypt. David's reference to cleansing with hyssop reminds us that it is the blood of Jesus Christ which cleanses us from all sin.

God looks at our heart. People look at actions that stem from what is in our heart!

Read Psalm 51:8-12 God will always hear a sincere prayer of confession and answer it with forgiveness and restoration.

There are many sad consequences when a believer sins, but one of the worst is the loss of fellowship with God. You can observe David's deep anguish over his broken fellowship with God. David remembered what happened to King Saul, that God had taken his Spirit away from Saul and given it to David. So David prayed in Psalm 52:11 "Do not cast me from your presence or take your Holy Spirit from me." God does not remove his Holy Spirit from sinning believers today. When the Holy Spirit enters a believer at salvation, he never leaves him. David had not lost his salvation, but had lost the joy of his salvation. What does he ask God to do in Psalm 52:12? *Restore the joy of his salvation and grant him a willing spirit to sustain him.*

Psalm 130:7b

"...with the Lord is unfailing love and with Him is full redemption."

The difference between fellowship and relationship

Your relationship with your parents is parent-child. No matter what you do, you will always belong to your parents. Sometimes you may quarrel with your father or mother, and your fellowship with one of them is broken.
Once we accept Christ we belong to God and will always have a relationship with him, but sin can break our fellowship with him.

Read Psalm 32:3-4. David tells us how he felt before he confessed his sin and was forgiven.

"When I kept silent, my bones wasted away through my groaning all day long. For day and night your hand was heavy upon me; my strength was sapped as in the heat of the summer."

Discuss the word picture here. He was drained of energy. Even night time would not let him escape his misery. He was like a wilted plant in the heat of the summer. He could not receive nourishment from God because of his broken fellowship.

Read Psalm 32:1-2, 5 for the **good news**! *"Blessed is he whose transgressions are forgiven, whose sins are covered. Blessed is the man whose sin the LORD does not count against him and in whose spirit is no deceit. Then I acknowledged my sin to you and did not cover up my iniquity. I said, "I will confess my transgressions to the LORD"- and you forgave the guilt of my sin.*

For the believer in Christ who has no unconfessed sin in her life and is walking in fellowship with God, there are many benefits of the Christian life, and we see some of those in Psalm 3 and 32.

- *We have a clean slate and new beginning.*
- *Our joy returns.*
- *We experience the fruit of the spirit. (Gal. 5:22-23)*
- *We can pray to God and he will hear us. (Psalm 32:6a)*
- *God will protect and deliver us. (Psalm 32:6b-7)*
- *He will direct our path. (Proverbs 3:5-6)*
- *He will instruct us. (Proverbs 3:8)*
- *He surrounds us with his love. (Psalm 32:10)*

Hopefully our responses to God's goodness and mercy and forgiveness will parallel those of the psalmist David. He promised to tell others what God had done for him. Psalm 51:13-15. *Then I will teach transgressors your ways, so that sinners will turn back to you. Deliver me from the guilt of bloodshed, O God, you who are God my Savior, and my tongue will sing of your righteousness. Open my lips, Lord, and my mouth will declare your praise.*

ILLUSTRATION

Illustration: Think of the biggest zit you have ever had. Think how sore, red and swollen it was. What a relief it was when you popped it and all the nasty infection came out and the swelling went down. What a relief when we **allow** God to "pop" our hearts and squeeze out the sin and clean out the guilt.

There are three ways we can deal with sin, and these three ways have very different outcomes.

1. We can cover up our sins, practicing deceit and lying about them. When we do this, we lose God's fellowship.

2. We can confess our sins. Confession brings relief, freedom, forgiveness and a new beginning.

3. We can conquer our sins by yielding continually to the power of the Holy Spirit within us.

Self Examination

At this time, give students a separate sheet of paper. Spread them out and instruct them to ask God to reveal to them any unconfessed sin in their lives and to list these sins on the paper. When your time period is up read 1 John 1:9 "If we confess our sins, he is faithful and just and will forgive us our sins and purify us from all unrighteousness." Ask students to wad up their papers. Now burn them all together.

At this time, you may give the students a bar of soap with 1 John 1:9 written on it. I call this "The Christians bar of soap!"

LESSON 14

SEPARATED, SATURATED, SITUATED
Psalm One

To prepare: Have a dictionary available. Have a plant that shows a good root system and a dead, dry plant.

The name "Psalms" comes from the Septuagint (the Greek translation of the Old Testament) where it originally referred to stringed instruments such as the harp and lyre, and later it referred to the songs that were accompanied by these instruments. The traditional Hebrew title means "praises", even though many of the psalms are actually prayers.

The Psalms were written as songs and were the hymnal for the Israelites. Their compilation probably spanned several centuries.

The Psalms were written in the form of poetry, although they do not rhyme nor do they have a standard meter like our poems today. The Psalms fall into several general categories some of which are:

- Hymns of praise. (For God's majesty and attributes.)
- Enthronement psalms. (These celebrate the Lord as King over the nations and over the whole world.)
- Laments. (Here individuals are asking deliverance from sickness or from their enemies. Some laments were sung by a nation in times of crisis or distress.)
- Thanksgiving. (These psalms are to thank God for answered prayer and praise him for his saving help.)
- Royal psalms. (These were sung for or by the present king.)
- Confessions of confidence in the Lord, often in spite of seemingly bleak circumstances.
- Songs of Zion. (These focus on the Holy City, Jerusalem, and the worship in the temple there.)
- Liturgical. (These psalms were used primarily in public worship.)
- Messianic. (These psalms foreshadow the coming of Jesus Christ and his work on the cross.)
- Instructional psalms. (These tell us how to live.)
- Wisdom psalms. (These reflect on the meaning of life and the wisdom of God.)

Psalm 1 is called a wisdom psalm and presents two opposite ways to live. This kind of presentation is seen in different ways throughout scripture. Some examples are as follows:

- Galatians 6:7-8 *"Do not be deceived: God cannot be mocked. A man reaps what he sows. The one who sows to please his sinful nature, from that nature will reap destruction; the one who sows to please the Spirit, from the Spirit will reap eternal life."*

- Matthew 7:24-27 *"Therefore everyone who hears these words of mine and puts them into practice is like a wise man who built his house on the rock. The rain came down, the streams rose, and the winds blew and beat against that house; yet it did not fall, because it had its foundation on the rock. But everyone who hears these words of mine and does not put them into practice is like a foolish man who built his house on sand. The rain came down, the streams rose, and the winds blew and beat against that house, and it fell with a great crash."*

- Matthew 7:13-14 *"Enter through the narrow gate. For wide is the gate and broad is the road that leads to destruction, and many enter through it. But small is the gate and narrow the road that leads to life, and only a few find it."*

⊏ With God or Without God? ⊐

There are two ways to live—with God or without God, as righteous people or as wicked. Psalm 1 makes this dichotomy very clear. It tells us that either we are blessed or we are perishing. Read Psalm 1.

God wants to bless his people! He wants us to be recipients and channels of blessing, but he has given us certain conditions for receiving blessings. God enjoys blessing your life, but you must be "blessable." Certainly, we desire and delight in being blessed by God. What does it take for us to be in a position to receive God's blessing?

We must be ***separated from the world.*** The world is anything that separates us from God or causes us to disobey him. Separation is not isolation but contact without contamination.

Ask students to give an example of what the last statement means.

Psalm 1:1 *Blessed is the one who does not walk in step with the wicked or stand in the way that sinners take or sit in the company of mockers,*

Being blessed involves having discernment, avoiding the steps that lead to sin. Sin is usually a gradual process. Notice the gradual decline of the sinner in verse 1.

He is _walking_.   (considering sin)

He is _standing_.   (contemplating sin)

He is _sitting_.   (becoming comfortable in sin)

Becoming worldly is *progressive*. It happens by degrees. We make friends with the world; we become spotted by the world; we love the world, become conformed to it and end up condemned with it. Lot is an example of someone who became worldly. He looked toward Sodom, pitched his tent toward Sodom and then moved into Sodom. As a result, he lost everything.

To be blessed, we must not only be separated from the world but we must also be ***saturated with the Word***. What you delight in will direct your life, so be careful what you enjoy.

Psalm 1:2 *but whose delight is in the law of the Lord, and who meditates on his law day and night.*

He delights so much in God's word that he *meditates* on it day and night. We saturate ourselves with the Word by meditating on it. Meditation is to the spirit what digestion is to the body. When we meditate on the Word, we allow the Spirit of God within us to "digest" the Word of God for us. So, not only do we delight in the Word, it becomes a source of spiritual nourishment for us. One dictionary defines "meditation" as "to think in view of doing." We can study our Bible to get information but then we need to "meditate" on how to relate it to our life. We study to serve; we meditate to live. Study can bring growth to our mind, but meditation brings growth to our inner being.

Psalm 1:3 *That person is like a tree planted by streams of water, which yields its fruit in season and whose leaf does not wither—whatever they do prospers.*

Discuss the word picture of a tree drawing nourishment from a nearby stream.

A tree is a blessing. It holds soil, provides shade and homes for birds and squirrels, and produces fruit. The godly are like trees, with root systems that go deep into the spiritual resources of God's grace. But, sadly, many professing Christians are not like trees but like artificial plants that look like the real thing but are not. Others are like cut flowers with no roots. They may be beautiful for a while, but they will eventually die.

A tree must have roots to live. The question we need to ask ourselves is, "Where are our roots?" The most important part of our lives is our root system. It determines our nourishment, and it also determines our stability and strength when the storms come and the winds blow.

"When we plant a tree, we select the spot where we want it and the type of tree best suited for that location and for the purpose we had in mind. God knows where He wants to plant us, and He has a purpose in planting us there. It may not be the place of our choice, but it is the place of His choosing." Millie Stamm, *Meditation Moments,* (Zondervan Publishing Corporation, 1967 P. 70)

We only bear fruit when we have roots, and we must draw upon spiritual resources to bring forth fruit in due season. *Where* we place our roots is of paramount importance. The person God can bless is **situated by the waters**.

We must be:

Separated from the world.
Saturated with the Word.
Situated by the waters.

Only as we grow our roots deeply into the spiritual resources of God's grace will we produce fruit. *Talk to the students about "growing in Christian maturity." Just as it takes a long time for a tree to reach maturity, so it is with our Christian walk. Their beginning faith is like a little acorn planted in the ground. It takes a lot of "outside" influence, deep roots and nourishment for it to grow into a strong oak and reach full growth.*

Psalm 1:4 *Not so the wicked! They are like chaff that the wind blows away.*
Show students a dry, dead plant.

We must be careful not to be like Christians who are dry and withered and depend upon their own resources. They are like "chaff" which has no roots, produces no fruit, and is blown about by any wind of doctrine.

Have a dictionary handy. 1: the seed coverings and other debris separated from the seed in threshing grain 2: something comparatively worthless Merriam Webster's Collegiate Dictionary – 10th ed., 1993.

Psalm 1:5-6 *Therefore the wicked will not stand in the judgment, nor sinners in the assembly of the righteous. For the LORD watches over the way of the righteous, but the way of the wicked leads to destruction.*
Ask students to compare the tree and the chaff.

Contrast tree and chaff and you will see the difference between the godly and the ungodly. The godly receive blessing but the ungodly receive judgment. The ungodly reject the Word of God and will perish without hope. How tragic that anyone is perishing when Jesus offers abundant life! The psalm starts with "blessed" and ends with "perish." The choice is ours.

Read Psalm 92:12-14 for a beautiful parallel passage.

"The righteous will flourish like a palm tree, they will grow like a cedar of Lebanon; planted in the house of the Lord, they will flourish in the courts of our God. They will still bear fruit in old age, they will stay fresh and green."

WHAT IS CHAFF?

Chaff is:

HOW DO I LIVE THE CHRISTIAN LIFE?

How did you enter the Christian life? *By faith.*

How can you live the Christian life? *By faith.*

Read Galatians 3:3 *Are you so foolish? After beginning by means of the Spirit, are you now trying to finish by means of the flesh?*

It is crucial to know how to enter the Christian life, but it is also important to know how to live it once you have entered it. The issue of how the Christian life is to be lived can be settled by answering one key question: how did you enter the Christian life? Did you receive the Holy Spirit by the works of the law or by faith?

How a person begins determines how he ends. The Christian life is of one nature. It doesn't change midstream. A cow is always a cow. A calf doesn't grow up to be a horse. It would be foolish to believe that the Christian life is of one nature at its beginning but that it changes its nature as it goes along. A person lives the Christian life the same way he entered the Christian life—by faith from start to finish.

Some believers choose bondage rather than liberty! Some people call this **legalism.** *Look this word up.* What is there about legalism that would lure a Christian into turning from grace to law?

Mary Love Eyster shares, "I was so foolish and ignorant for 30 years. I believed that old adage that 'God helps those who help themselves.' I thought the way to live the Christian life was to do my best and only ask God for help when I couldn't handle things. I thought the less often I had to bother God for help, the more pleased He would be with me. I had a spiritual beginning, because that's the only way to enter the Christian life, but I was trying to live for God in my own strength and wisdom. I felt I was unsuccessful because I hadn't tried hard enough yet, and I kept pushing to try to do better."

Legalism appeals to the flesh. The flesh loves to be religious and to obey laws, to observe holy occasions, even to fast, so it can boast about its religious achievements. There is nothing wrong with these activities if the attitude is right, but in legalism these things are done to glorify the person rather than God.

Legalism also appeals to the senses. The legalists do not want to worship God in spirit nor walk by faith. They want to walk by sight and by other senses as well. People who depend upon legalism can measure themselves and compare themselves with *others.*

We should always use Jesus as our standard of measure. Even on the cross he said, "Father forgive them."

Guilt is a primary tactic of legalists as they try to take away the joy we have in our freedom in Christ. Legalists are also experts at *intimidation.* They can give you a disapproving stare or point a finger your way.

It is very important to read our Bibles, attend Sunday school, pray and witness. These things are the backbone of the Christian life, but they can be done in such a mechanical way that they prove to be ineffective. It is more important to meet with Jesus when we pray than just log in so many minutes of quiet time. We want to apply what we are reading in God's word rather than just reading so many verses. We also want to allow the Holy Spirit to do his thing in our lives instead of just following the lives of other Christians (including your parents).

Keep our eyes on him and not each other!

"You're not the boss of me!"

My grandchildren like to tell each other, "You're not the boss of me." The matter of the Holy Spirit is like this: will you take charge of your own life or will you allow the Holy Spirit to work in and through your yielded life? ***And be the boss of you!***

Would you like to have the Holy Spirit living the Christian life through your body today? WHO IS THE HOLY SPIRIT?

Person, Guide, Counselor, Teacher

In John chapters 14, 15 and 16, Jesus referred to the Holy Spirit as "He", not it. Throughout the Bible, we see that the Holy Spirit is God Himself. What are the following attributes of the Holy Spirit?

Hebrews 9:14 *He is eternal.*

Luke 1:35 *All powerful.*

Psalm 139:7 *Omnipresent*

1 Corinthians 2:10-11 *Omniscient*

Read John 14:16-17, John 15:26-27, John 14:26 and John 16:12-15 to discover more. Record your findings below.
John 14:16-17   He is a comforter who leads me into truth.
John 15:26-27   He is a comforter and a source of truth.
John 14:26   He is a comforter and a teacher.
John 16:12-15   He will guide you into truth.

The Holy Spirit is Part of the Trinity

The first mention of the Holy Spirit is in Genesis 1:2. See also Genesis 1:26.
The Holy Spirit is an active part of the Trinity. He is the spirit of the Father (Matthew 10:20) and the spirit of his Son (Galatians 4:6). In John 15:26 we find all three persons of the Godhead (Trinity) mentioned.

Promise of the Holy Spirit

Old Testament

1 Samuel 16:13 *The Spirit of God came upon David at his anointing.*

Exodus 31:3 *The Lord told Moses that he had filled Bezalel with his Spirit and had given him great abilities.*

New Testament

Luke 1:35   *The angel told Mary that the Spirit would come upon her.*

John 16:7   *Jesus said it was best for us for him to go away so he could send the comforter.*

John 14:16   *Jesus asked God to give us a comforter.*

John 1:8   *The Holy Spirit will give power to testify.*

At Pentecost

Acts 2:14-17   *The Spirit will be poured out.*

Next to the importance of Christ's coming to earth is the coming of the Holy Spirit.

Have you ever tried to operate something electrical and finally found out that the reason it wasn't working was because you had forgotten to plug it in? Don't you imagine that the angels watch us and are astounded by our efforts to make life work without plugging into God's power? I am amazed at myself when I forget that the infinite, personal Spirit of Christ lives within me to guide my life and give me power. His Spirit enables me to do God's will, to show God's attitudes, and to fulfill God's purposes. But I have to stay plugged in through prayer, reflection on God's word, and complete reliance on his power—not my own!

LESSON 16

SHARING MY FAITH

"Therefore go and make disciples of all nations, baptizing them in the name of the Father and of the Son and of the Holy Spirit, and teaching them to obey everything I have commanded you. And surely I am with you always, to the very end of the age." Matthew 28:19-20

Tell students that they will be putting their testimony together this week. Next week they can take turns sharing with the group!

In Lesson 12, we discussed spiritual gifts, and one of these was evangelism. We described evangelism as a "burning desire" to see lost people introduced to Christ. Even though we do not all have a "calling" to evangelism, we are all instructed to carry out the great commission of Christ given to us in the Matthew 28 passage.

Do you find it hard to share your faith? Why do you think this is so?

Who would love to silence you?

Why is it important, even crucial, that we share our faith with others?

Undoubtedly, someone shared the story of Christ's love with you. What difference did it make in your life? What difference could it make in someone else's life? What are you waiting on?

MY TESTIMONY

James 1:5 Ask God to guide you!

A simple outline could be:

- My life before I accepted Christ.
- How I accepted Christ.
- My life after accepting Christ.

My life before Christ:

>You might tell of areas in your life that were "self centered" or in need of Christ's touch.   Did you feel that something was "missing" in your life? Were you drawn to believers by their characteristics?   Always be truthful when sharing.

How I accepted Christ:

>Explain exactly how you received Christ. The person you are sharing with should be able to accept Christ by your clear example.   Some people remember an exact time and place when they made their decision to trust Jesus Christ with their lives.   Some even celebrate their "spiritual birthdays." Others may have made their decision as children, knowing in their hearts there was a time they wanted Jesus controlling their lives but were unable to recall an exact date or time.

If you're not certain whether you have invited Jesus into your heart, you can make certain by asking him to be your Savior:

A—Admit you are a sinner and ask for forgiveness (Romans 3:23, 1 John 1:9);

B—Believe in Jesus as your Savior and become a child of God by receiving him (John 3:16, John 1:12);

C—Confess that Jesus is Lord and choose to follow him daily (Romans 10:9, Luke 9:23)!

My life after accepting Christ:

How has your life been different? Do you have a strong desire to walk closely with God and to denounce sin? What about your prayer life?

It is important to write your testimony down and to practice sharing it. This will give you confidence because you will know what you are going to say and how you want to say it. You will want to avoid negativity, stereotyping and mentioning church denominations in your story.

You are not alone when you are sharing. Jesus promises that the Holy Spirit will give you power when you witness according to Acts 1:8. He also promises that your efforts will not be in vain according to Isaiah 55:11.

John 14:6 tells us that Jesus is the only way to God. People are hungry for him and need him in their lives. Your friends need forgiveness. Strangers you meet need to hear of God's love. A life controlled by God's love and producing much fruit is the best life that there is!

MY TESTIMONY

<u>Opening sentence, attention getter, or thought provoking question:</u>

<u>Before I became a Christian I lived and thought this way:</u>

<u>How I received Christ:</u>

After I received Christ these changes took place:

Closing remarks (could share a favorite verse):

LESSON 17

TESTIMONY SHARING

As the leader you should be the first to share your testimony. Take the time to be prepared; remember you are their example!

Ask God to speak through the power of the Holy Spirit as you share what He would want you to say. Be yourself and be truthful. If you are nervous, it's ok; that should be expected. (Remember who does not want you to learn to share!) Philippians 4:13, "I can do all things through Him who strengthens me."

Write the names of those in your group below and leave space for comments. Let them know what touched you most about their testimony and give advice on what they could improve.

THE TWENTY THIRD PSALM

Read the 23rd Psalm.

David wrote this psalm. As you think back over his life, what do you think inspired him to write this beautiful psalm? *Peace and assurance.*

Let's examine each verse together. Read and record what you think the following verses mean.

Psalm 23:1 *"The Lord is my shepherd, I shall not want."*

Remember where David began his incredible life, in the pastures, shepherding sheep. What are some of the needs of sheep?

They are: protection, grooming and feeding. When they stray, they need to be returned to the flock.

How are we like sheep?

Isaiah 53:6 *"We all, like sheep, have gone astray, each of us has turned to his own way."*

Don't we tend to stray into situations that get us into trouble? We allow problems and irritations to steal our joy and peace and disrupt our sleep. We are vulnerable to predators from both the natural world and the supernatural world.

Do we need a shepherd? Yes, indeed! Psalm 23 tells us that the Lord is our Shepherd. Psalm 100:3b says, *"We are his people, the sheep of his pasture."*

What does our Shepherd do for us?

Philippians 4:19 *"And my God will supply all your needs according to his glorious riches in Christ Jesus."*

Psalm 23:2 *"He makes me lie down in green pastures; He leads me beside quiet waters."*

What do you think the psalmist meant by "green pastures" and "quiet waters"? *The pastures and waters provide a picture of peace, protection, provision, refreshment, tranquility and serenity.*

What invitation is God giving us in John 7:37b? *"If anyone is thirsty, let him come to me and drink."*

How can we do that? *Give our hearts to him. Read and study the Bible. Pray. Obey his commands.*

Have you ever heard of a cast sheep? Sheep have short legs and heavy bodies. Sometimes when they lie down, especially if there is an indentation in the ground, they will roll over in such a way that makes it impossible for them to get up without help.

Have you ever felt like a cast sheep?

Who has helped you up?

What can we do to help each other up?

Psalm 23:3 *"He restores my soul. He guides me in paths of righteousness for his name's sake."*

Why would our souls need restoring? *Our sinful attitudes and actions break our fellowship with our heavenly Father.*

How does God restore our souls?

1 John 1:9 *"If we confess our sins, he is faithful and just and will forgive us our sins and purify us from all unrighteousness."*

Matthew 11:28 *"Come to me, all you who are weary and weighed down with heavy burdens, and I will give you rest."*

Why would he lead us in paths of righteousness for his name's sake? How would you feel if you did something that caused your family shame? Would you want to do things that would bring shame or disgrace to the name of our Heavenly Father?

Our Good Shepherd defines for us the path of righteousness in the Bible. God's word tells us the things we should do and things we should not do. When we become Christians we get on the right path, but sometimes we stray from the path. Then we need to confess our sin and repent and ask God to put us back on the path of righteousness. Our Shepherd helps us stay on the right path.

Psalm 23:4 *"Even though I walk through the valley of the shadow of death, I will fear no evil, for you are with me; your rod and your staff they comfort me."*

Once we have accepted Christ, the Holy Spirit comes to live within us and will never leave us. We will not take even one step in the valleys, the hard times, of life alone. Our Shepherd will be right there with us.

Matthew 28:20b gives us some reassuring words from Jesus. *"And surely I am with you always, to the very end of the age."*

Psalm 23:5 *"You prepare a table before me in the presence of my enemies. You anoint my head with oil; my cup overflows."*

What do you think of when you hear the word table? *Families and friends often eat together. God's provision for us and for fellowship.*

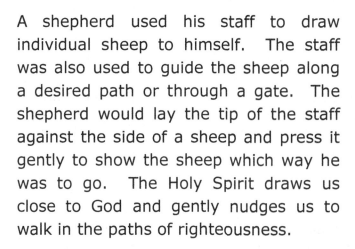

A shepherd used his staff to draw individual sheep to himself. The staff was also used to guide the sheep along a desired path or through a gate. The shepherd would lay the tip of the staff against the side of a sheep and press it gently to show the sheep which way he was to go. The Holy Spirit draws us close to God and gently nudges us to walk in the paths of righteousness.

The rod was the shepherd's weapon with which he protected both himself and his sheep. The shepherd also used his rod to correct wandering sheep, just as God's word corrects us when we stray away from obeying God.

The anointing of oil has different purposes. Insects of all kinds can become annoying and upsetting to the sheep in the summer. The antidote is for the shepherd to rub the sheep's heads with a specially prepared oil mixture.

There are many aggravations and irritations that buzz around us, upsetting us and stealing our peace and joy. Just as oil is applied to the sheep, God's Holy Spirit must continually anoint us to counteract the frustrations of life and bring us peace and joy.

The antlers of the rams were greased so when they fought their horns would slide off each other rather than interlocking and causing injuries. The Holy Spirit will keep us from "locking horns" with other people and make us kinder and gentler in our relationships.

Another purpose of the oil was to heal wounds. The Holy Spirit comes alongside to comfort and heal us when we have been wounded by the unkindness of others or the trauma of tragic events.

What might an "overflowing cup" represent at the end of the verse? *Plenty, provision, generosity, God's abundant gifts.*

Share how God has blessed you.

Psalm 23:6 *"Surely goodness and love will follow me all the days of my life, and I will dwell in the house of the Lord forever."*

It is easy to see that God's goodness and mercy are following us when all is going well in our lives. But when there are health problems, financial difficulties, divorces, tragic events, or the deaths of people we love, it is much harder to see God's goodness and mercy, but it is still there. It is not our circumstances that reveal how much God loves us – it is the cross! Never forget this: "Jesus loves me! This I know, for the Bible tells me so."

The place which God has prepared for those who love him will be beautiful and wonderful far beyond anything we can imagine. It will be a place of "no mores" – no more sickness, sorrow, pain, death, tears, or struggles. The best part is that God will live there with us and so will Jesus and our loved ones who die in Christ. No matter how hard our journey to heaven may be, the destination will be worth it all!

This week, take notice of the many ways your Shepherd, Jesus, is "providing and guiding" in your life.

LESSON 19

THE PROVERBS 31 WOMAN

Read Proverbs 31:10-31

Have you ever known someone who seemed to have it all together and made you feel intimidated? Have you looked at beautiful movie stars and felt inadequate? When you hear the description of the Proverbs 31 woman, how do you feel?

Some Bible scholars believe that the Proverbs 31 woman is a compilation of great womanly virtues rather than one single, specific woman. Whether she is one woman or many, she is the personification of wisdom. It is one thing to talk about virtues like wisdom, faith, integrity, courage, etc. in the abstract, but it is another thing to see these qualities lived out in a specific person, in other words, personified.

Mark Twain once said, "Few things are harder to put up with than the annoyance of a good example."

If we want to see **faith** personified, we can look at the life of Abraham. Can you give an example of faith in Abraham's life?

God told him to leave his home in Ur, and Abraham gathered up his family and left. Abraham was also willing to sacrifice Isaac as God had instructed, believing that God would raise him back to life.

If we want to see **integrity** personified, we can look at the life of Daniel. Can you give an example of integrity in Daniel's life?

Daniel refused to eat certain foods even though he was a captive in a foreign land and was being fed the king's best.

If we want to see **courage** personified, we can look at the shepherd boy David. Can you give an example of courage in David's life?

He fought the giant, Goliath, with only a sling shot.

If we want to see **evangelism** personified, we can look at Paul. He suffered so much for the spreading of the gospel, yet continued to preach. What did this eventually cost him?

His life.

If we want to see the personification of **wisdom**, we can find it in the Proverbs 31 woman. Let's look at her life and see how she lived out some of the qualities that are found in wise people.

Proverbs 31:10

A wife of noble character is worth more than _rubies_. We might call her a jewel of a woman!

A good name is worth more than what? *Riches, gold and silver.*

$$\left[\text{Proverbs 22:1} \right]$$

A good name...

Proverbs 31:11-12

Her husband has full _confidence_ in her! He knows he can trust her.

She brings him good not _harm_, all the days of her life.

What are some ways a woman can bring a man good and not harm?

She can praise him and build up his confidence. She can take care of him. She can bring him honor and show him respect. She can be a companion to him.

The Proverbs 31 woman is not lazy at all.

Read Proverbs 31:13, 15, 17-18 and 27.

Record a few of her accomplishments:

She works with her hands. She gets up early and provides food for her family and her servant girls. She works hard with her strong arms. Proverbs 31:27 sums her up, "She watches over the affairs of her household and does not eat the bread of idleness."

The Proverbs 31 woman is a woman of excellence. What she does, she does well and thoroughly. She doesn't settle for something just because it's easy, but goes for quality!

Proverbs 31:11, 12 and 29

"Her husband has full confidence in her and lacks nothing of value…she brings him good, not harm, all the days of her life…Many women do noble things but you surpass them all."

DEFINE: NOBLE

You might say she is a woman of "integrity."

Some descriptions might be: grand, magnificent, stately, elevated, moral, honorable, etc.

The following is a question asked in the book <u>The Day America Told the Truth</u>, written by James Patterson and Peter Kim, 1991.

What are you willing to do for $10,000,000? Two-thirds of Americans polled would agree to at least one, some to several, of the following:

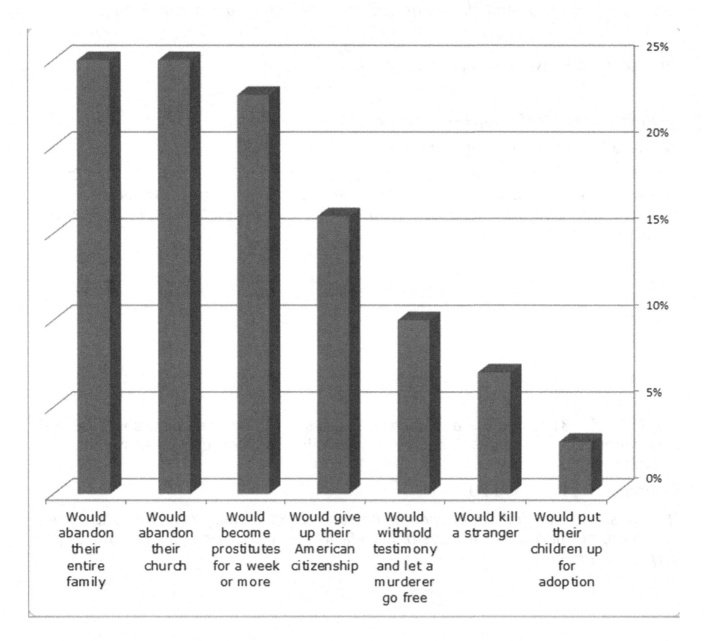

The woman we are talking about would not compromise her integrity at any price.

She takes care of things because she should, it is right and she loves her family, not because she is trying to impress others.

Her good character reflects well upon her husband.

Write Proverbs 31:23 and explain. *"Her husband is respected at the city gate, where he takes his seat among the elders of the land."*

Have you ever heard the saying, "Behind every great man is a great woman?" Your influence on a man can be immense.

> "Behind every great man is a great woman."

The Proverbs 31 woman also trains her children up in the way in which they should go.

Proverbs 31:26 *"She speaks with wisdom, and faithful instruction is on her tongue."*

Napoleon Bonaparte was quoted, "The future destiny of the child is always the work of the mother. Let France have good mothers, and she will have good sons." Have you ever heard the saying, "the hand that rocks the cradle is the hand that rules the world?"

The Jukes Family

In 1875 Richard L. Dugdale announced his study of the Jukes family in the annual report of the Prison Association of New York. His findings were later published in the Carnegie Institute of Washington by Arthur H. Estabrook. Max Jukes was an unbelieving man, and he married a woman of like character who lacked principle. Among his known descendants, over 1,200 were studied. Three hundred and ten became professional vagrants; 440 physically wrecked their lives by a debauched lifestyle; 130 were sent to prison for an average of 13 years each, 7 of them for murder. There were over 11 who became alcoholics; 60 became habitual thieves; 190 were public prostitutes. Of the 20 who learned a trade, 10 of them learned the trade in a state prison. They cost the state about $1,500,000 and they made no contribution whatever to society.

The Edwards Family

The following is taken from a 1925 reprint of Winship's report on the descendants of Jonathan Edwards. This was about the same era as Max Jukes. Jonathan Edwards was a man of God, and he married a woman of like character. Three hundred of their descendants became clergymen, missionaries, and theological professors; over 100 became college professors; over 100 became attorneys, 30 of them judges; 60 became authors of good classic books; 14 became presidents of universities. There were numerous giants in American industry who emerged from this family. Three became United States congressmen, and one became the vice president of the United States.

Do you think the way you raise your children is important?

Does it matter?

The Proverbs 31 woman is a good business woman.

Proverbs 31:16, 18a and 24. She makes the most of her financial opportunities.

"She considers a field and buys it; out of her earnings she plants a vineyard...She sees that her trading is profitable...She makes linen garments and sells them, and supplies the merchants with sashes."

Over and over in Proverbs we have been encouraged to be kind to the poor, and the wise Proverbs 31 woman does just that.

Proverbs 31:20 *"She opens her arms to the poor and extends her hands to the needy."*

The Proverbs 31 woman plans ahead for the needs of her family.

Proverbs 31:21-22, 25 *"When it snows she has no fear for her household; for all of them are clothed in scarlet. She makes coverings for her bed; she is clothed in fine linen and purple. She is clothed with strength and dignity; she can laugh at the days to come."*

Discuss what this scripture means. *This woman demonstrates her strength and efficiency by building a strong and secure household. She takes care of economic responsibilities so her family is safe from disaster. She lays up reserves so that her family will have plenty. She enjoys the present and faces the future with confidence and optimism.*

Proverbs 31:30 *"Charm is deceptive, and beauty is fleeting; but a woman who fears the Lord is to be praised."*

A woman's good character and virtue can grow stronger and more attractive as her youthful beauty fades. A wise woman spends her time and effort in cultivating these instead of trying to hold on too tightly to her physical beauty. What are some ways you can "grow" your character and virtue?

Remember Proverbs 1:7, "The fear of the Lord is the beginning of wisdom"? The Proverbs 31 woman was praised because she feared the Lord. This was her most important characteristic.

Proverbs 31:28, 31 *"Her children arise and call her blessed; her husband also, and he praises her." "Give her the award she has earned and let her works bring her praise at the city gate."*

The fear of the Lord was the secret of the staying power of the Proverbs 31 woman. She received the grace that his Spirit supplies. The greatest worth of the virtuous woman is her devotion to the Lord.

Jesus is the greatest example we will ever have, but who of us mortals could ever hope to achieve what Jesus achieved? By ourselves, the situation is absolutely hopeless.

Galatians 2:20a, *"I have been crucified with Christ and I no longer live, but Christ lives in me.*

2 Corinthians 4:7, *"But we have this treasure in jars of clay to show that this all-surpassing power is from God and not from us."*

There is no way we can live the Christian life, but we can experience it, because God loves us so much he is willing to live it in and through us through the wisdom and power of his Holy Spirit.

> The Proverbs 31 woman is not just a good example for us to try to copy. God didn't put her in the Bible to frustrate and discourage us. The Proverbs 31 woman is a picture of what God wants to do through us as women, if we allow his Holy Spirit to control us.